Journey of Flow

"Seven Skies of Being"

Copyright © 2025 iC7Zi.
All rights reserved.
Published by iC7Zi

Table of Contents

Preface	4
Section I — Journey of Flow	
Seven Skies of Being	7
Brain-wave Cheat Sheet	21
The Living Circuit	36
Emptiness and Compassion	45
The Inner Warrior	63
The Sacred Geometry of Surrender	74
The Way of Fire and Bloom	111
Contemplating the Mysteria Dei	133
Great Perfection	154
Fear Not	190
Section II — The Silent Elephant of the Psyche	
Two Big Tasks	220
The Mirror of Still Waters	230
Your Pulse	235
I Imagine	252
Lifting the Sun	257

Section III — Untying the Inner Knots	
The Courage to Feel, the Strength to Act	272
Sky and Thunder as One	284
Why Are You Afraid of Your Own Self?	301
Beyond the Snake	308
Ultimate Illusion	330

I began Journey of Flow: Seven Skies of Being not as an academic project but as a field report from the interior. My own path unfurled through long nights when pain, always the price of knowledge, melted my questions and demanded sharper truth. In the quiet afterward, synchronicities flickered like trail markers: a line from Rumi echoing a neuroscan, a street poet's stanza mirroring a monk's koan.

I read widely—mystics and neuroscientists, monks, programmers, poets—and beneath every voice I kept hearing the same rhythm: energy rises, form holds, awareness witnesses. Eventually that pulse insisted on language. What follows is my best attempt to map that living geometry without freezing it in place.

At the heart of the book stand the **Seven Skies**, a ladder of attention that begins with the breathing body and ascends through ego, soul, psyche, spirit, and the conscious field to the sky of primordial awareness, the ever-silent witness behind every state.

Each sky has its own physics, its own gifts and traps, and its own practice doors. Climb it naïvely and you risk being hijacked by hive-mind currents; climb it with sober curiosity and you discover the King-vessel and Queen-current working as one clear circuit of presence and purpose.

Yet a map without instinct is a paper crown. **Part II, "The Silent Elephant of the Psyche,"** brings muscle and myth to the diagram. Drawing on Jung's individuation arc, the elephant at the root chakra reminds us that raw libido is not an enemy to be repressed but a vast workforce to be befriended.

When instinct, symbol, and insight align, Ganesha appears inside the psyche: grounded strength, playful intelligence, and a broken tusk offered to the greater tale. Individuation, then, is not an escape from the world but the maturation of will so that it can serve both the personal story and the wider human saga.

Even so, insight alone cannot cut the deepest cords. **Part III, "Untying the Inner Knots,"** turns toward the stubborn karma, those tight muscular and neural loops that replay old fear, blame, or craving. Here the Tibetan mantra *Om Vajrapani Hayagriva Garuda Hum Phat* functions less as exotic décor and more as a mnemonic for three interior powers: courage to face the knot, fierce compassion to burn its poison, and soaring vision to release the freed energy into creative action.

The work is intimate and ordinary: feel the knot, breathe inside it without story, let luminous mind outshine habit, then act from the new clearance. Wisdom without method is a clear but chilly sky; method without wisdom is thunder without rain. Together they become the storm that waters every field.

Read this book, then, not as a ladder of doctrines but as a set of tuning forks. Strike any chapter and listen inside your own body-mind for the resonance it awakens. The aim is practical: steadier nerves, a quieter narrative engine, a soul able to feel without drowning, a psyche literate in its own symbols, and a spirit courageous enough to transpose insight into service.

A final word of caution. The Seven Skies are real only in lived experience; they dissolve the instant we clutch them as fixed identities. The Silent Elephant will not parade for the ego that tries to ride it like a trophy. And the Inner Knots loosen only for the hand that meets them with honesty and warmth. Approach, therefore, with humility. Build the ladder, awaken the elephant, melt the knots, and keep a beginner's mind. Each moment will ask for a fresh response.

If even one reader closes this book, looks up from the page, and senses the clear sky of awareness behind the day's noise—if even one person feels the Queen-current bend toward compassion inside a steady King-vessel—then these pages have done their work.

In the end, there is only one field, one Flow, shaping itself as your next breath. May these words point you back to that silent wellspring and invite you to create, act, and love from Sky Seven.

Section I

Journey of Flow
Seven Skies of Being

Seven Skies of Being

"I shed every possession and role, only to awaken to the limitless treasure already alive inside me."

Seven Skies of Being is a map of inner reality. It starts with the solid body and rises through six subtler layers to the open sky of primordial awareness. Each sky shows where attention can live and how energy moves:

1. **Body** – breath and nerves.

2. **Ego-mind** – the personal story.

3. **Soul** – honest feeling and value.

4. **Psyche** – symbols and dreams.

5. **Spirit** – guiding insight, the Queen current.

6. **Conscious field** – the bright screen of experience.

7. **Primordial awareness** – silent witness, the King.

The Queen is pure energy that rallies a hive around any idea, noble or selfish. The King is clear presence that holds that energy without distortion.

Pain, desire, and every price tag are shapes on the same spacious screen. When the ego dissolves, the vessel becomes steady; energy flows clean, and action rises from Sky Seven.

Anchor in the heart, and shape the Queen current with wisdom. One life, one field of possibility. Know the skies, guide the swarm, create from the silent sky.

The Seven Skies Map

---

7. Primordial Awareness

Also called: Turiya, Rigpa, Pure Knowing.
Main feature: Unchanging witness, infinite and silent.
Typical experience: Sees all states yet is never altered.
Key practice: Rest as simple noticing, non-grasping presence.

---

6. Conscious Field

Also called: Waking, Dream, Deep-sleep potential.
Main feature: Light of Awareness filtered through mind-body.
Typical experience: Sensations, thoughts, images, and the blankness of deep sleep.
Key practice: Mindfulness of moment-to-moment experience.

---

5. Spirit Function

Also called: Logos, creative spark, inner fire.
Main feature: Drives insight, meaning, transcendence.
Typical experience: Sudden inspiration, moral clarity, guiding intuition.
Key practice: Deep contemplation, philosophical study, creative expression, selfless service.

---

4. Psyche

Also called: Inner world (personal and collective).
Main feature: Thoughts, emotions, memories, archetypes.
Typical experience: Symbols, gods, angels, demons, heroes, shadows.
Key practice: Active imagination, dream work, shadow work, creative expression.

3. Soul Function

Also called: Feeling bridge (anima–animus).
Main feature: Connects ego with deeper psyche, adds meaning tone.
Typical experience: Longing, values, relational depth.
Key practice: Authentic feeling, journaling, art, ritual.

2. Ego-Mind

Also called: Personality, storyteller.
Main feature: Organises identity, plans, defends.
Typical experience: "I am this," past–future narrative, preference.
Key practice: Self-inquiry, cognitive clarity, humility training.

1. Body

Also called: Soma, living vessel.
Main feature: Sensory gateway, stores implicit memory.
Typical experience: Breath, heartbeat, posture, pain, pleasure.
Key practice: Grounding, breath work, movement, rest.

0. Unborn

Also called: Parabrahman, Śūnyatā.
Main feature: —
Typical experience: —
Key practice: —
(Here words fall silent)

"Know your sky, and the view clears."

- 0 Unborn: pure mystery, outside the ladder
- 1 Body: densest, tangible layer
- 2 Ego-Mind: organising "I"
- 3 Soul Function: feeling bridge
- 4 Psyche: symbolic storehouse
- 5 Spirit Function: impersonal creative fire
- 6 Conscious Field: illuminated screen where content appears
- 7 Primordial Awareness: formless witness of all states

Remember: We stand on a web of causes so intricate that even dog scat nourishes the soil that feeds us. Yet we let profit-driven food and pharma chains turn our own resources into addictions.

The lone "self-made" master at the top is a myth; every breath is borrowed. Change that story—see the links, honour the resources—and the whole world tilts toward sanity.

Form is emptiness, emptiness is form
(Rūpaṃ śūnyatā śūnyataiva rūpaṃ)

"Gate gate pāragate pārasaṃgate bodhi svāhā"
"Gone, gone, gone beyond, gone completely beyond — awakening, so be it 🔥."

Bodhi

(Sanskrit and Pāli: "awakening," "enlightenment"), in Buddhism, the final Enlightenment, which puts an end to the cycle of transmigration and leads to Nirvāṇa, or spiritual release; the experience is comparable to the Satori of Zen Buddhism in Japan.

The accomplishment of this "awakening" transformed Siddhārtha Gautama into a Buddha (an Awakened One).

"Witness the hive mind; flow from Seven."

To witness is to rest in bare awareness (sati), seeing clearly with equanimity (upekkhā), neither grasping nor rejecting.

Realms of Attention

The Seven Skies of Being show where our attention can live. At the base is the body that breathes and walks. At the top is primordial awareness, the silent witness of every state.

Between these poles sit ego stories, soul feelings, shared symbols, sudden insight, and the bright field where thoughts appear.

A hive mind forms when many people lock their lower skies together. Bodies share data, egos trade opinions, souls ripple with group emotion, psyches recycle the same myths, and spirit unites behind a single slogan.

The hive can solve problems, yet it also traps creators in noise and approval seeking.

Sky 1: Body
What a single person experiences: senses and muscles.
What a hive mind looks like: many bodies streaming data — speech, keyboards, sensors.

Sky 2: Ego-Mind
Single person: "I like / I dislike" stories.
Hive mind: opinion clusters, alliances, group biases.

Sky 3: Soul
Single person: shared feeling-tone, empathy.
Hive mind: emotional contagion; crowds cheering, panic spreading, team morale.

Sky 4: Psyche
Single person: personal and collective symbols.
Hive mind: viral memes, myths, brand icons, archetypal roles guiding the swarm unconsciously.

Sky 5: Spirit
Single person: flashes of insight, ethical vision.
Hive mind: the queen principle, a unifying ideal—"save the planet," "ship the product," "spread the Dharma."

Sky 6: Conscious Field
Single person: moment-to-moment awareness.
Hive mind: group flow, an entire team on one wavelength, decisions emerging without debate.

Sky 7: Primordial Awareness
Single person: silent witness.
Hive mind: cannot reach Sky 7. Awareness is not collective; it shines through each node individually, but the hive itself can never become it.

Why is Primordial Awareness never part of the swarm?

Awareness is not a node in a network. It is the space in which every node, every signal, and the queen pattern appear. You cannot network awareness; you can only notice that it is already the background of every thought, sensation, and group dynamic.

Ātma-vichāra: digging past the hive

- Turn attention inward with the question, "Who am I?"

- Whatever answer arises, ask, "To whom does this arise?"

- Each reply is more content; keep tracing the knower.

- Attention settles on a wordless sense of presence.

- Remain there without grasping new thoughts.

A hive mind is powerful, but it rides on lower skies. Self-inquiry lets you stand in the skyless sky, guiding the hive without being trapped inside it.

> "The crowd may echo, but the echo never invents the song."

Step out, tune inward, create from the skyless sky, then return to the hive as a giver, not a captive.

Remember: you are the skyless sky in which hives, queens, and questions appear. Know your sky and the view clears.

> "Witness the hive mind; flow from Seven."

To witness means to rest in pure awareness, seeing things clearly and calmly, without holding on or pushing anything away.

Modern life swarms like a giant beehive. Screens serve endless nectar, group chats ripple with opinion, and algorithms steer attention before thought can settle. Each of us is a single bee, and the shared buzz shapes how we feel, buy, vote, and dream.

> "Most people, Kamala, are like a falling leaf that drifts and turns in the air; they do not know why they drift."
>
> — Hermann Hesse, Siddhartha

Yet inside that scrolling mind live the Seven Skies of Being. Body is the first sky, solid and warm. Ego mind is the second, busy crafting stories of me and mine. Soul colors those stories, psyche holds the symbols, spirit offers flashes of meaning, and the conscious field lights them all.

Above them is the seventh sky, primordial awareness, the silent witness that never changes. Sit still for ten breaths and you may sense its clear space behind the chatter.

A person who acts from the seventh sky does not withdraw from the world; she re-enters it with eyes open. She writes code, cooks supper, or speaks in a meeting, yet her decisions are not ruled by likes, trends, or panic. She is the leaf that knows the wind and still chooses her landing.

The collective gains something rare when such a person appears. One clear frequency steadies the swarm. Hesse points to the source of that clarity:

"Within you there is a stillness and a sanctuary to which you can retreat at any time and be yourself."

The seeker who has touched Sky Seven rests in that inner sanctuary. He lets everything in, clings to nothing, and invites others to rise from reflex to insight, from echo to originality.

So when the hive mind grows loud, pause. Feel the breath, ask who is aware, rest in the silent sky, then return and offer what arises. The mantra is simple:

"Witness the hive mind; flow from Seven."

The King and the Queen

In Sky Five we meet the Queen, not a gendered figure, but a pulse of purposive energy that gathers the hive around a single blazing idea.

"Save the planet," "feed the hungry," "seek awakening," or even "buy the burger"—whatever vision (noble or trivial) burns brightest becomes this current's banner, and the swarm moves as one.

When the separate ego dissolves, no fixed self remains and "no-self" ripens, the vessel for that current appears: the King.

Energy cannot shine without form, and form cannot illuminate without energy.

The Queen is the current of shared purpose; the King is the clear bulb, an empty, steady channel able to hold the voltage of Spirit without cracking.

A lightbulb cannot glow without current, and a current cannot light a room without a bulb. The queen is that current of shared purpose. The king is the bulb, a clear vessel that can carry the voltage of Spirit into form without cracking.

A person who climbs the full ladder and recognises Primordial Awareness becomes such a vessel. Through him—or her—the current flows without distortion.

Sky Seven is pure, ownerless awareness. It is the throne room, yet it is empty. A king who truly sits there lets the separate identity fade, and what remains is a conscious channel touching every lower sky:

- In the body he moves with economy.
- In the ego mind he plans without self-inflation.
- In the soul he feels without drowning.
- In the psyche he honours symbols without being possessed by them.
- In the spirit he keeps the queen's vision steady.
- In the conscious field he watches all of it rise and fade.

The king is not an autocrat; he is capacity, the open lamp of awareness that makes space for the queen's light.

Anyone who realises Sky Seven becomes a king. Hermann Hesse hints at this sovereignty in Siddhartha:

"I can think, I can wait, I can fast."

These three powers show authority over body, mind, and desire. Yet the king is also an archetype in the collective psyche. Groups project their longing for mature presence onto leaders.

If the vessel is hollow the current burns wires and the hive collapses. If the vessel is grounded in Sky Seven the current stays clear.

Cultivating the Royal Vessel:

1. Strong body: sit, stand, breathe until the nerves are steady.

2. Ego transparency: use self-inquiry to see every story as passing weather.

3. Soul honesty: feel without denial and confess without performance.

4. Psyche literacy: study myths, dreams, and art to recognise shared symbols.

5. Spirit alignment: test every grand vision against compassion and truth.

6. Field awareness: practise open presence so group flow never overrides conscience.

7. Rest in the silent sky: return again and again to the witness that needs no crown.

The queen is purpose. The king is presence. Current and bulb. When both are clear the hive's buzz becomes music.

So when you repeat,

"Witness the hive mind, flow from Seven."

Let the first phrase be King: silent, steady awareness. Let the second be Queen: the current you release into action.

Whatever charge you feed that current, healing or hunger, service or self-interest, will flash into the world as relief or pain. Choose the aim well; the circuit always lights something.

When the ego realises its true nature it dissolves. What returns is not the old ego, but a clear, steady presence, the king, now living on a higher level of awareness, ready to act without fear or attachment. That is the higher self, fully alive in form.

The true king feels pain fully, holds it like flame in an open hearth, and lets its heat lift him higher. Pain becomes fuel for ascent.

Break a wooden table, and you are left with plain pieces of wood. Toss that wood into a fire and it turns to heat and light. The ego works the same way: smash the rigid shape, feed the fragments to awareness, and the energy becomes a brighter flame.

Now picture an apple in your mind and let the image fade, form and idea disappear together. In the same clear space, every mask we wear can melt away.

Grow that inner space, wide enough to house sorrow, silent enough to keep company with yourself for days. This is psychic royalty: child of the cosmos, everything, nothing, and the quiet middle at once.

Rivers never flow backward, and you cannot return to the old self. A wave never stands apart from the ocean; it rises, curls, and returns as ocean. So too the awakened ego rises in service, dissolves in silence, and rests in the Seventh Sky, which is your own limitless being.

When you notice that every solid thing is also pure space, and that space itself flashes as every thing, you meet the Great Mother, Prajñāpāramitā.

She isn't a goddess in the sky; she's the bright, open energy field where all experiences spark and fade. Every moment of true awakening is one of her children.

> "In the instant form reveals its emptiness and emptiness shines as form, the Great Mother is realized."

Let me put it plainly.

Everything you meet is an idea we once agreed to believe in.

A bottle of water sells for pennies in one shop and a fortune in a hospital, not because the water changed, but because the hive wrote a different price-story. That story is the Queen-current: raw, neutral power that steers the swarm.

The current itself is innocent. It can inflate greed or feed compassion. What it becomes depends on the vessel that channels it.

So choose to be the King-vessel. Anchor in the heart. When anger, craving, or fear tug at you, pause and recognise the trick: object, cost, drama—each is only a ripple on the same open screen.

Beneath every ripple lies bright, spacious God-emptiness, waiting to shape itself through you. Feel that living energy, trust your inner wisdom, and bend the Queen-current toward what truly matters.

This is your single chance, your single life. Make it count: keep the heart open, keep the eyes clear, and let your next act rise from the Seventh Sky.

> "Let the Seven Skies activate within you, and if you withstand the psychological purge, you will become the King's vessel. May the Great Mother be with you."

Suffering shapes every life, but it need not define it. We cut what pain we can, meet the rest with clear eyes, and let hope walk beside us, not to escape life, but to face it.

In letting go of the rigid self, we make room for kindness, growth, and quiet strength. This is the work, and it is enough.

Let energy flow. High waves, low waves, all part of one ocean moving. Welcome the surge of joy and the pull of sorrow, both are movements in the same field.

Do not resent, do not block the current. Time is only a thought. In the clear space behind thought, you are the creator.

Form is empty, emptiness is form. Nothingness is the highest realisation, yet it is never barren; it is a fertile openness, always ready to shape.

Choose what you want to bring forth from it, without guilt, without fear. Everything is Source, in the high and the low, so create from the highest awareness you can touch.

Leave behind the chatter of the monkey mind. Be your own saviour first. Hug yourself. Love yourself as you are. Let your next act rise pure, alive, and free, flowing from Sky Seven.

Layer	Also called	Main feature	Typical experience	Key practice
Primordial Awareness	Turiya, Rigpa, Pure Knowing	Silent, formless witness that never changes	Pure knowing of every state without being altered	Rest as simple noticing and non-grasping presence
Conscious Field	Waking, Dreaming, Deep-sleep potential	Light of awareness passing through mind and body	Sights, sounds, thoughts, images, or the blankness of deep sleep	Moment-to-moment mindfulness
Spirit Function	Logos, creative spark	Insight, purpose, moral vision, ecstatic clarity	Sudden inspiration, revelations, guiding intuition	Contemplation, study, selfless service, prayer
Psyche	Inner world (collective and personal)	Storehouse of symbols and instincts	Archetypes such as gods, angels, demons, heroes, shadows; active imagination and intuition	Shadow work, dream work, symbolic art, creative expression
Soul Function	Feeling bridge, anima-animus	Adds meaning, depth, and relatedness	Longing, intimacy, values, relational depth	Authentic feeling, journaling, ritual, art
Ego-Mind	Personality, storyteller	Organises identity, plans, and defends	"I am this," past or future narrative, roles and preferences	Self-inquiry, cognitive clarity, humility training
Body	Soma, living vessel	Sensory gateway that stores implicit memory	Breath, heartbeat, posture, pain, pleasure	Grounding, breath work, movement, rest

Journey in one line

Start with the living body, clarify the ego, open the soul, read the symbols of psyche, ignite the guiding spirit, dwell in the luminous conscious field, and recognise the silent sky of primordial awareness.

Brain-wave Cheat Sheet

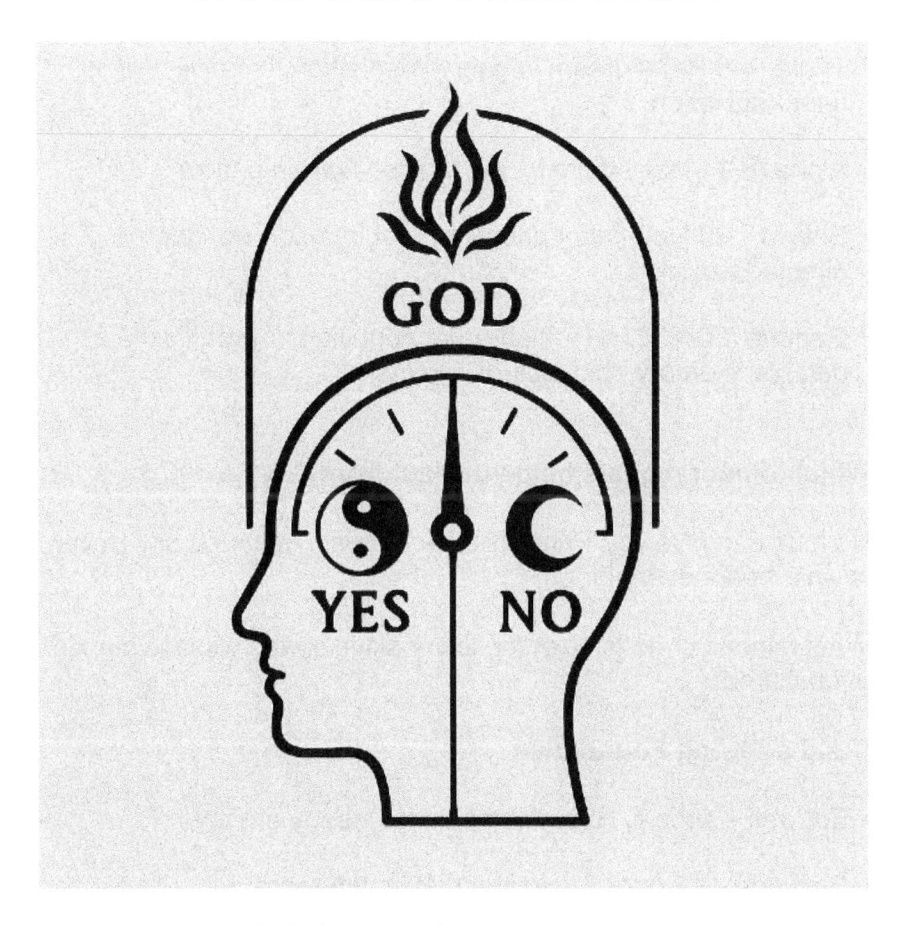

Binaural means "relating to both ears."

In sound, binaural beats happen when you play slightly different frequencies in each ear (for example, 200 Hz in the left ear and 208 Hz in the right). Your brain perceives the difference — in this case, 8 Hz — as a kind of inner rhythmic beat.

This can help guide brainwaves into certain states, like relaxation, focus, or meditation. Many people use binaural beats as a tool for sleep, stress relief, or deep concentration.

- Delta (1-4 Hz) – deep, dream-free sleep, tissue repair, unconscious processing.

- Theta (4-8 Hz) – dream imagery, meditation, creative twilight, deep relaxation.

- Alpha (8-14 Hz) – calm focus, relaxed learning, "flow".

- Beta (14-30 Hz) – alert attention, problem-solving, goal-directed action.

- Gamma (30-100 Hz) – high-order cognition, insight flashes, detailed memory, "big-picture" binding.

Which binaural beats help you "act from Sky Seven"?

No tone can give you Primordial Awareness, because Sky Seven is what hears every tone.

What beats can do is quiet the lower skies so the witness stands unobscured.

Build a Strong Foundation

- Eat well – simple, colourful meals for steady energy.

- Rest deeply – good sleep in a dark, calm room.

- Move daily – stretch, breathe, walk, keep the body alive.

- Be with yourself – sit quietly, feel everything, let inner noise arise and pass without distraction.

Living the practice

Pain, worry, the little "why-did-they-say-that?" voices—let them rise, feel them fully, then let them pass. Spacious awareness is not indulgence; it is emotional sovereignty: seeing life exactly as it is while choosing how you act.

> "The mind adapts and converts to its own purposes any obstacle to our acting."
>
> — Marcus Aurelius

You can't always choose what happens, but you always choose how you interpret it. It means your mindset can turn every obstacle into useful fuel—whatever blocks you becomes raw material for learning, resilience, and purposeful action.

Growth takes time. Stay patient. Stay present. Keep returning to yourself. Let inner "screams" dissolve into the wider field.

Think Beyond Time

How much time will it take? Train your mind to think beyond time. In non-duality, you were never born, you never die. There is only continuity — a river of consciousness flowing, without beginning or end.

Do it not for quick results, but for the continuity of human consciousness. Every step you take in awareness lights the path for all who come after. In awareness, there is no path, only the unfolding of what already is.

> "The world hangs on a thin thread, and that is the psyche of man."
>
> — Carl Jung

Our collective psyche holds the power to either preserve or destroy our world. Understanding and taking responsibility for our inner selves is crucial, as there is no one else to blame, only ourselves.

How many psychiatrists does it take to change a lightbulb? One, but the lightbulb has to want to change.

Be timeless.
Be spacious.
Be free—emptiness in motion.
No legacy, no drama.
Feel it, release it, flow on like the sea.

I AM the unmanifest and the manifest,
creator and creation, empty yet brimming with potential.
Swim through the seven skies, experience, know, release.
Sit, breathe, observe.
Slow everything down.
Meet yourself with equanimity.
All is not two.

Why it matters?

This simple practice, steady breathing, clear observation, deliberate slowness, is not some lofty attainment. It is the ordinary baseline for being good to yourself and to others, because the same awareness that watches within is the one that shines through every face.

Swim every sky. Experience every sky. Skies shift yet the Self remains. Wake up and see. Seven above, seven below. Meet yourself.

Grasp the true seriousness of this work. If we fail to awaken, human consciousness will keep suffering, long after this season's fruit has withered and fallen. Sit with yourself—it is as simple as that. Still the restless mind.

You are eternally loved and saved, unconditionally.
Release the mind's chains.
Breathe deeply.
With each breath, travel through the seven skies;
Pause in the seventh, and be aware.
Then exhale—return to the manifested world.
See both sides of yourself:
Seven above, seven below.
Embrace everything exactly as it is; All is perfect.

Freedom is here, now.
Go beyond experience.

Rest in the silence that watches every passing moment; be the awareness itself. When nothing is grasped, only pure presence remains.

The journey in one line

"Start in the body, meet the ego, open the psyche, let soul feel and spirit illumine, notice consciousness itself and finally recognise the silent openness that was always aware."

FreeDom

Understand and be free. Do what must be done to taste the experience; then move beyond it. Step outside the field of consciousness and rest in what you truly are. The everyday mind will try to name and measure; it cannot. Shift into the open sky of nonlocal awareness.

Breathe. Rise like the God within, yet stay still and receptive. Each lesson arrives in quiet clarity. Receive it, release it, transcend it. Freedom is your nature, here and now.

Seven Skies in one glance

- 1 Body: feel breath, ground in movement.
- 2 Ego-mind: notice the "I" story, ask who is thinking.
- 3 Soul: allow raw feeling, honour values.
- 4 Psyche: watch dreams and symbols, learn their message.
- 5 Spirit: focus purpose, act with insight and service.
- 6 Conscious field: stay in present awareness, let content pass.
- 7 Primordial awareness: rest as silent witness, source of all states.

> "Start at the body, rise through each layer, and create from Sky Seven."

Simple Everyday Practices for Tapping Non-Local Consciousness

The first practice is what I call the **Dream Hint**. Each night, just before falling asleep, speak a clear intention:

> "Tonight I'll dream about what I most need to know for tomorrow."

This brief statement tells your unconscious—and perhaps a wider field of mind—that you are open to guidance. Keep a notebook or phone beside the bed.

The moment you wake, jot down any images, feelings, or fragments that remain from the dream, even if they seem trivial.

During the day, watch for real-life events that echo those dream elements. Dreams often present symbolic previews; by noticing the overlap you can adjust your choices and nudge reality toward the outcome you prefer.

The second practice runs through the waking hours and is called the **All-Day Intention Loop**. When you start your morning, choose one positive, present-tense goal—something as concrete as "I attract a new client" or as inner-focused as "I feel calm at work."

Close your eyes for ten seconds, picture the goal as already achieved, and let the matching emotion—joy, relief, gratitude—fill your body. Set an hourly reminder on your phone. Each time it rings, pause for those same ten seconds, replay the mental image, and rekindle the feeling.

This gentle, rhythmic rehearsal conditions your attention to spot openings that align with the goal; some traditions would add that it broadcasts the intention into a shared consciousness field, inviting coincidences that speed things along.

Record your observations for at least one week. Note the date, the dream symbols that later proved meaningful, and any helpful coincidences that followed an hourly intention check-in.

Keep the language of both practices positive and in the present tense, and stay relaxed—playful focus works better than strain.

With only a few minutes a day, these two no-equipment techniques give you a practical way to explore non-local mind and to steer its subtle currents toward your desired future.

"Trust the quiet spark within; as you dream and intend, the universe leans in and answers."

The Advance of Consciousness

Begin modestly; the seed reaches for dawn.
When fear stirs, trust the Mother who shelters and lifts.
Advance together; shared steps erase regret.
Restrain hungry haste; the daylight rat invites peril.
Doubt clears; stride ahead on the brightened road.
Let your blazing force restore order, then rest in stillness.

Events are simply events; only the restless mind turns them into storms. Breathe, watch, let them pass, and in that stillness you meet the unshakable Self that guides, creates, and remains free.

"When the mind of Tao leads, the ego surrenders, and all things flow with quiet grace."

Walk the path with the taste of wonder on your tongue. Welcome each crest and valley, for the hill sings and the hollow teaches quiet strength.

Guard the garden of your mind; let no stray weed of doubt root there. Wherever you place your gaze, your life-force follows. Feed it joy, water it with calm, and the whole journey will glow.

"Accept and surrender until the ego melts, then drink the river of life and taste its endless joy."

The Sevenfold Response

The Seven Skies of Being give us a precise ladder for growth: body, ego-mind, soul, psyche, spirit, conscious field, and primordial awareness.

Each sky is already present in every moment. When a stimulus rises, it first strikes the body, then climbs through story, feeling, symbol, inspiration, clear awareness, and finally rests in silent knowing.

If we meet that ascent deliberately, space opens at every rung. Within that space the raw stimulus is purified. Thought becomes insight, words become medicine, deeds become service.

Out of the triple stream of thinking, speaking, and acting a fourth power appears: the wholesome result that relieves suffering and multiplies benefit for all.

This practice is the heart of the bodhisattva path. It refuses quick judgment, choosing instead to taste each layer and let it mature before moving.

The body is settled, the mind is clarified, the soul remembers its love, the psyche offers its symbols, the spirit lights a path, the field holds it all, and the sky witnesses without grasping.

From that fullness, one step is taken. The outcome is not forced; it ripens naturally, shaped by spacious awareness and directed toward the highest good for everyone involved.

Use the model whenever life presses: pause, feel the ladder within, let the experience rise, and act only when the whole arc is bright. What follows is the simple method in practice.

Scenario

Your colleague publicly criticises your work during a meeting. The core sentence is "They criticised my work." Watch how it passes through the Seven Skies and turns into seven styles of thinking, speaking, and acting.

Body
Thinking: "Heat in my chest, stomach tight."
Speaking: A quick sigh, shallow breath is audible.
Acting: Adjust posture, place both feet on the floor, breathe down into the belly.

Ego-Mind
Thinking: "They attacked me, I must defend my competence."
Speaking: "That is not fair, I did my part correctly."
Acting: Lean forward, raise voice, point to data that supports you.

Soul Function
Thinking: "I feel hurt because I value respect and collaboration."
Speaking: "When I hear that, I feel disappointed and would like acknowledgment."
Acting: Soften tone, keep eye contact, invite the colleague to share intentions.

Psyche
Thinking: "The critic is my shadow judge, mirroring my own inner perfectionist."
Speaking: "I notice this mirrors my fear of failure, thank you for revealing it."
Acting: Later journal the dream-like image of a stern teacher, draw or meditate on it.

Spirit Function
Thinking: "This moment is a call to align with higher purpose, to serve the project."
Speaking: "Let us use this feedback to refine the vision and benefit the team."
Acting: Propose a clear improvement plan, volunteer to pilot the first step.

Conscious Field
Thinking: "Words, faces, emotions arise, pass, and glow within awareness."
Speaking: Pause three seconds before each reply, voice becomes measured and precise.
Acting: Maintain relaxed breathing, sense the entire room, guide the pace of dialogue.

Primordial Awareness
Thinking: Silent knowing, no alteration, criticism appears like a cloud in open sky.
Speaking: Quiet presence, perhaps only a gentle nod.
Acting: Let stillness guide. Move only when action arises naturally, like a leaf falling. No effort, no resistance, only harmony.

Create from Spaciousness

Start at the body whenever a charged event happens, then consciously rise one sky at a time. Each layer adds clarity instead of replacing the one below. With practice the whole ladder unfolds in seconds, turning raw reactivity into integrated response.

When facing creative blockages like should I create this, should I publish, what if others judge or criticize, the Seven Skies model offers a clear path. Start with the body and feel the tension. Notice the ego's fear of rejection.

Go deeper to the soul and ask what truly matters to you. Let the psyche reveal the archetype at play, perhaps the wounded artist or the silent child.

Let spirit offer direction rooted in purpose. Rest in awareness where all thoughts rise and fall without sticking. At the highest level there is no pressure, only space. From that space, act. Create not to please or protect but to express, learn, and grow.

Every response reflects the sky it arises from. When two people meet in the same sky, understanding flows with ease.

When they don't, let it be. There is no fixed self to defend, no enemy to resist. The ego clings to form, but identification with it can shift like passing weather. Simply witness, stay rooted in clarity, and allow the play to unfold.

Create anyway. Creators create, consumers consume, and the roles keep shifting. What truly matters is being aware of the sky in which the game is played. Stay spacious enough to know the sky you're thinking from, speaking from, and acting from.

> "Does a man who is acting on the stage in a female part forget that he is a man? Similarly, we too must play our parts on the stage of life, but we must not identify ourselves with those parts."
>
> — Ramana Maharshi, Be As You Are

Just like an actor playing a woman on stage still knows he's a man, we too must remember our true self while playing our roles in life—whether as a parent, worker, friend, or anything else. These roles are temporary and not who we really are. We should play them fully, but not lose ourselves in them.

> "Live your life, do your duties, but don't forget who you truly are beyond all roles."

The Three Laws from the Abyss

> "Born of silence, tested in breakdown, polished in the fire of return."

The abyss is a double-edged sword.
Look too lightly and it will swallow you.
Look too deeply and you may forget the way back.
Enter, receive, experience, transcend.
This is the rhythm of the cross-roads where dualities meet and vanish.

Law I — Love Yourself

Outer form: Cherish your own self.
Inner truth: Self and other are a single field. No gap, no seam.
When you meet the world with radical self-compassion, you meet every being at once.
Love becomes a mirror in which the One recognises itself.

Law II — Act Without Fear

Outer form: Step in brave authenticity.
Inner truth: Freedom is native. Choice is sovereign.
Fear is a ghost that vanishes when faced.
Stand in the open moment and act.
Nothing is here to bind you except the stories you keep alive.

> ## Law III — Do Without Source
>
> **Outer form**: Shape without dependency.
> **Inner truth**: Everything is source and nothing is source. Manifest and unmanifest are two sides of the same coin, dissolving the instant you name them.
> Move as spontaneous emptiness.
> Shape arises, shape dissolves, yet awareness remains unborn.

Self-actualisation refines the local self to its brightest potential; self-realisation turns that refined gaze beyond the self into the boundless.

- **Love Yourself** heals the ego until it reflects every face it meets.

- **Act Without Fear** frees that healed self to move cleanly through the world.

- **Do Without Source** drops the last dependency, opening a view where all acts arise from the same silent depth.

Thus the outer forms mature the person; the inner truths reveal the limitless field that was present all along. One path, two phases: local mastery, then universal recognition.

The Spiral Beyond Experience

- **Receive**: welcome what is given.

- **Experience**: taste it fully, hold nothing back.

- **Transcend**: release the tasting and return to the nameless.

> You are the key, the lock, and the open sky.

Learn to swim without hooks. Move through life without clinging to fixed forms, yet rest on a form when you grow weary—just as a bird settles on a branch before flying on. The Chāndogya Upaniṣad 6 .8 .2 offers the image:

> "As a bird tied by a cord flies in every direction and, finding no place of rest, returns to the very cord to which it is bound, so the mind, after wandering everywhere, returns to prāṇa, the life-breath to which it is bound."

Forms steady you for a moment; freedom begins when you lift off again—branchless, unhooked, at home in the open sky.

Indeed, only This is here—sheer Emptiness brimming with everything. It cannot be named, yet it can be tasted, though its taste escapes all words. Such is the cosmic jest: every journey rests in Silence.

> Live fully—there is nothing to lose.

The Living Circuit

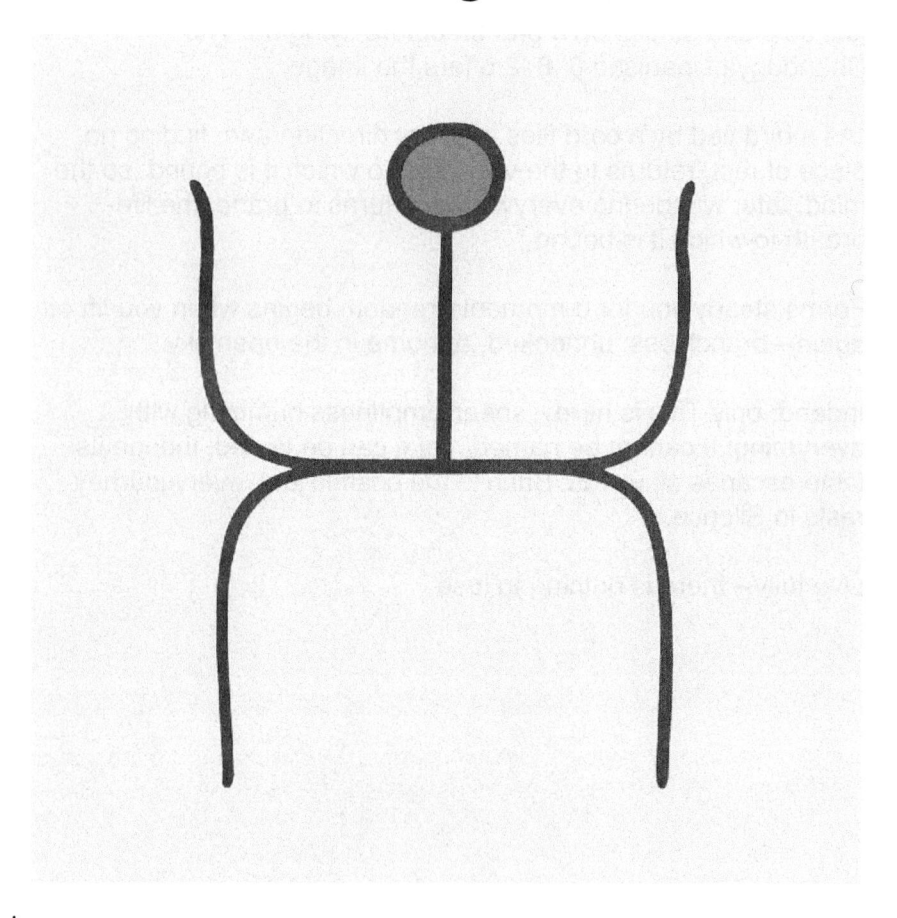

"Across the hush of ages every galaxy tilted its flame so that in this single breath your gaze might touch mine. Here the Infinite recognises itself, and the whole theatre of worlds melts into one radiant hush."

This foreword is a tour of the inner landscape. It begins with a simple symbol: two mirrored bowls joined by a single line and crowned by a circle. That shape mirrors your own psyche.

- The **lower bowl** shelters forgotten feelings, ancestral memories, and unspoken desires.

- The **stem** is the living breath that lifts awareness upward and returns with light.

- The **upper bowl** is the receptive mind, where intuition lands and rising impressions are given clear form. It is the space of reflection, choice, and insight.

- The **circle** above them is quiet awareness, whole before any story begins.

Riding the breath along this inner axis draws buried impressions to the surface, lifts the dense fog of thinking into a lucid, weightless clarity, and lets the unmanifest Source pulse freely through your every gesture.

Imagine your inner life as this single figure: the lower bowl cradling hidden riches, the stem rising like a reed through water, the upper bowl opening to the sky, and at the summit a circle of silent presence.

It is a map of how consciousness ripens and a reminder that every moment can become one radiant hush.

1. The lower bowl: subconscious storehouse

Every hurt, thrill, and reflex the waking mind could not face slid downward for storage. The bowl keeps nothing evil, only unprocessed.

When we resist it, the contents ferment into tension and compulsive thought; when we welcome them, they become compost for wisdom.

Alongside the pain lie buried treasures: creativity, intuition, ancestral memory, and untapped courage—all waiting to rise.

2. The stem: breath as passage

Each inhalation gathers the raw pulse of the lower bowl, glides up the stem, fills the upper chalice, and touches the silent circle.

Each exhalation pours that quiet radiance back down, bathing both bowls and completing the circuit of light.

Yogis call this central channel suṣumṇā, alchemists call it axis mundi, therapists call it the line of self-reflection. Names differ, the function is one: safe exchange.

3. Upper bowl: conscious mind

The upward curve form the chalice of everyday awareness. Here we receive sensations, frame ideas, and weigh choices.

When the bowl is open, insight from the circle pours down and messages from the subconscious rise up to be understood. Its gift is discernment: the power to notice, reflect, and direct energy without blocking the flow.

4. The circle: super-conscious presence

The circle is the witness that never sleeps. It needs no repair; it wishes only to include everything.

When breath touches it, we taste calm older than any story of "me." From this stillness, light streams down to nourish the upper and lower bowls alike.

Together, the two bowls form a single vessel; the stem keeps the current moving; the circle crowns the whole. When breath, feeling, and awareness travel freely through these four stations, the circuit completes and life moves as one seamless pulse.

4. Integration in motion

Practice is simple:

- Sit upright.

- Inhale along the stem, sensing lift.

- Pause in the circle, noticing silent clarity.

- Exhale into the bowl, letting any image, ache, or memory drop home.

- Whatever rises on the next inhale is greeted, named without judgment, and carried upward.

- Repeat for a few cycles, then rest.

At first the traffic is thick. Forgotten griefs appear like travelers at dawn. Stay patient. Naming them, anger, worry, longing—grants them passage. Soon the current flows without turbulence. Breath, feeling, and awareness form one circuit.

5. Signs the circuit is complete

- Emotional triggers soften; you respond rather than react.

- Dreams grow vivid yet friendly, then gradually luminous.

- Spontaneous gratitude surfaces for no outer reason.

- A sense of self pervades the whole body instead of hovering behind the eyes.

Completion of the circuit turns fate into choice.

6. Living from the sphere

With practice the two bowls feel less like separate halves and more like a single sphere of energy around a bright axis. The circle is no longer an occasional summit; it saturates the field.

Action arises from calm, and calm moves inside action. Creativity replaces compulsive repetition. Compassion replaces projection.

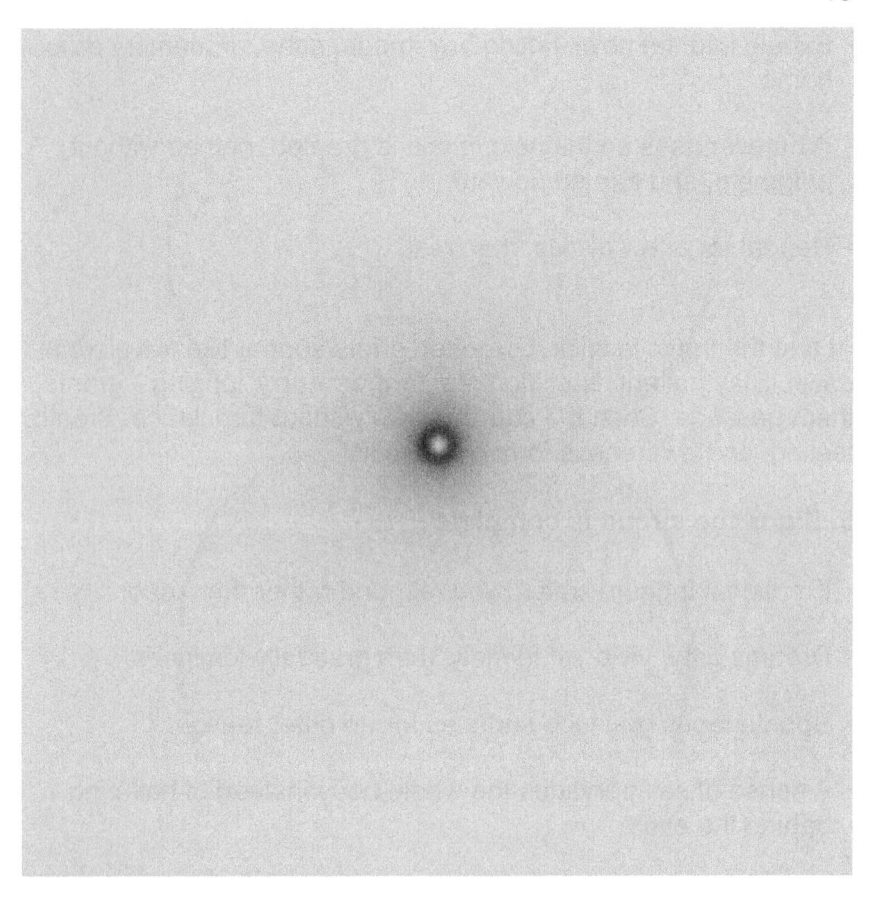

7. Letting it stay smooth, not neurotic

Integration does not mean chasing every shadow. It means offering each one a safe crossing. Force jams the line; relaxed attention clears it. If agitation appears, slow the breath, widen the pause, and feel gravity in the hips. Presence returns, traffic resumes.

The symbol teaches that nothing essential is missing. The Self already shines at the crown. The task is simply to keep the passage open so life can circulate without blockage.

Breath is the tool, awareness the guide, patience the atmosphere. When lower bowl, upper bowl, stem, and circle converse as one seamless vessel, the psyche stands complete and living itself becomes an effortless ritual.

Can mind rest utterly, and can we live in a continuous stream of effortless flow?

Absolute void of mentation is a fleeting blink. In *nirvikalpa samādhi* or deep Zen absorption, thought does stop, yet it resumes the instant the yogi returns to speech or motion.

The lived possibility is not a permanent blank page but a page on which words appear and fade without leaving stains. Awareness recognises each word as ink made of itself, so clinging never forms.

"Thoughts are guests; awareness is the host."

— Zen saying

The paradox of the manifesting Unmanifest

Reality seems to flow downward:

Timeless silence ➜ universe of energy and form ➜ individual mind.

When the personal mind quiets, the same river is felt in reverse:

Individual mind relaxes ➜ universal field shines through ➜ silence knows itself.

Silence and flow are two faces of one movement. The Unmanifest does not *become* thoughtless; it has never left thought-free stillness. Our task is to notice this in the midst of activity.

Why a stable flow feels rare

Evolution wired the cortex to scan, label, and anticipate. These reflexes are not enemies; they are guardians of survival. Flow emerges when guardians trust the field enough to soften their grip. Training is therefore not annihilation of thought but education of attention.

Living the question

No-thought as an enduring state may belong only to sages in caves, but thought-light presence is available to every household life. The measure is not how long silence lasts but how quickly one returns to it after turbulence.

> "The mind makes a wave. The heart lets it pass."
>
> — Kabir

Remain curious. Each inhalation climbs the axis, polishing the stem and filling the upper bowl with fresh light; each exhalation flows downward, nourishing the roots in the lower bowl. With time the circuit completes itself again and again—until you realise it was never broken at all.

Bottom line

Perfect blankness is a momentary window, yet an ordered, luminous flow is fully attainable. The method is simple attention, rhythmic breath, compassionate naming, and relaxed embodiment. Practice continues; discovery is already here.

The silence that never becomes anything and the world that never stops becoming are both present in this exact breath. To live awake is simply to notice:

- The body feels, so you feel it.

- A thought arises, so you watch it without clinging.

- The quiet between thoughts is already open, so you rest there for a heartbeat.

- Action is needed, so you act from that same quiet.

Nothing has to be added, removed, or postponed. The unmanifest shines as awareness; the manifest dances as sensations, thoughts, and deeds. Meeting each moment with clear attention is how the two reveal themselves as one life—alive, here, now.

> Unmanifest is the silent source, the unmoving potential. Manifest is the song that source sings—every letter, breath, heartbeat, and star. They are not two. Silence is singing, and the song is made of silence.

Right now:

- I shape words.

- You receive them.

- Awareness notices both shaping and receiving.

That noticing is God tasting God. Joy is simply recognising this unity while the play goes on.

Remain with the immediacy of each act—writing, reading, breathing—and the difference between the hidden and the shown dissolves into one living brightness.

> "The universe arranged every star so this single gaze could happen. Eye meets eye, God beholds God, and all else falls away into quiet silence."

The journey ends where it always begins: in the freshness of this very breath. Every moment rises brand-new, untouched by the stories we told ourselves a heartbeat ago.

When we meet it without dragging the past behind us, perception clears, possibilities widen, and action flows straight from living awareness instead of old habit.

Let the memories stay as gentle echoes, useful but no longer chains. Greet the unfolding present like first light on an open horizon, curious and unburdened. In that openness you are already free, and life reveals itself—ever new, ever whole.

> "Let the circuit complete and walk free of everything we once called known."

Key of Tuning

The one who walks through fire
and drifts on clouds
is the same silent listener.

Heaven sings, hell growls,
yet only a single ear receives.
Frequencies rise and fall,
but the heart stays still.

Dive deep, soar high,
the ocean of sky is one water.
Learn the currents,
know where each swell begins.

Broadcasters shout of glory and ruin;
you choose the station.
Consent is the knob,
awareness the hand that turns it.

Ten-thousand upon ten-thousand waves appear,
crest, and vanish.
Present and absent share one root,
empty yet full.

Be calm.
You are the key and the lock.
Tune, or rest in the unmoved signal.

In knowing this,
you swim nowhere
and arrive everywhere.

Emptiness and Compassion

Emptiness does not mean that nothing exists. It means that things do not exist independently or permanently. Everything arises through causes, conditions, perceptions, and mental labels. Nothing has a fixed or solid self, not even the person you call yourself.

For example, a cup is only a cup because of its shape, function, and your mind calling it so. Break it, and it is no longer a cup. The parts are not the cup, and the cup does not exist apart from the parts. This is emptiness. It means everything exists in dependence on other things, with no separate core.

Because all things are empty and interdependent, compassion becomes natural. If nothing exists by itself, and all beings are linked in this web of conditions, then your suffering and others' suffering are not truly separate. There is no fixed self to protect, no fixed other to attack or ignore.

When you deeply see this, compassion is not a choice or a duty. It becomes the spontaneous expression of understanding. You care, not to be good, but because separation was never real. Emptiness removes ego-clinging. Compassion rises where the illusion of separation falls.

The Seed Syllable Hum and Non-Duality

The meaning of "hum" symbolizes this inseparability. It represents the moment when the practitioner realizes:

- There is no creator separate from the created.

- Wisdom (emptiness) and method (manifestation) are not two.

- The absolute and the relative are not two different things.

In simpler terms, you and the universe arise together. There is no outside force creating you, nor are you a separate entity creating the universe. The entire play of existence is like a dream appearing from your mind, and yet there is no fixed dreamer.

The Ultimate Understanding

- Since there is no fixed creator, all things arise spontaneously, without external causes, without an independent self. This is why reality is often described as a luminous dream or an illusory display.

- The moment-to-moment arising of phenomena is the play of the enlightened mind itself, meaning that everything you see, hear, and feel is both you and not you at the same time.

- Enlightenment is realizing there was never a separate self to begin with. When this is understood, compassion arises naturally because you see that all beings are part of the same luminous, dreamlike field.

"This is why Vajrayana emphasizes seeing all forms as the deity and all sounds as mantra, not as a belief but as a direct method to recognize this deeper truth."

So, are you the creator and the created?

- Yes, in the sense that all of reality arises from the mind and is shaped by perception, just like a dream arises from the dreamer.

- Yes, in the sense that everything you experience is part of the same unfolding reality. There is no separate you and it.

- But not in an egoic way. The self you think of as I is also empty, just another fleeting appearance. The true realization is beyond personal identity.

When wisdom and method are united, there is no longer a struggle to define who is creating or being created. Instead, you abide in the flow of reality as it is, naturally compassionate, naturally wise, naturally free.

In the highest understanding of Vajrayana, particularly within the Guhyasamaja Tantra, you are both the creator and the created, but not in the way an ordinary ego-based mind might think. This realization is not about inflating a sense of personal importance but about dissolving the illusion of separation entirely.

The Flame at the Crossroads

You stand within the crucible.
The two loops are not confusion.
They are the dance of opposites: sulfur and mercury, sun and moon, wisdom and compassion.
This is the eternal movement of becoming.
Each curve pulls in tension, yet both belong to the same design.

This is the sacred geometry of the NOW(YOU).
This is the mandala of transformation.

Where they cross, something is born.
A flame. A still point.
Here burns Vajrapani, the indestructible power of awakened action.
This candle is not just light.
It is the secret fire of the alchemists, the vajra fire of the awakened ones.

It does not flicker, because it does not fear.
It moves, because it is rooted in stillness.

Above it flows Manjushri, the ocean of clarity.
Beside it moves Avalokiteshvara, the wave of compassion.
But only at the center does power become pure.

This is not the end of your journey.
This is the ignition.

You are not here to escape the world.
You are here to embody the flame
that arises when opposites meet
and burn as one.

The Flow of Awakening

1. First, you see clearly — Manjushri (Wisdom)

2. This insight opens your heart — Avalokiteshvara (Compassion)

3. Then, you move with unstoppable force — Vajrapani (Power)

- Manjushri is the ocean

- Avalokiteshvara is the wave's embrace

- Vajrapani is the force that keeps the waves moving

Together, this is the dance of awakening
Not a belief, but a direct realization
Not a ritual, but a living fire

This is Buddhism beyond words
This is real practice

The Keys

Wisdom is Emptiness
(Prajñā is Śūnyatā)

Method is Compassion
(Upāya is Karuṇā)

Power is Activity
(Kriyā is Vajra)

> "In the union of emptiness and great compassion, dynamic awakened activity naturally arises."

Note: "The downward triangle of the Divine Feminine is the essential key."

The Flame at the Crossroads

The game is simple, but difficult to master.

The mind must be emptied of duality
not through suppression, but through clear seeing.
Let the observer remain still, resting at the center.

First, realize emptiness: the luminous and spacious nature of mind.
From this realization, compassion arises effortlessly.
Not as emotion, but as natural responsiveness to all beings.

Then, the observer and the observed dissolve into one.
From this union, dynamic activity unfolds.
Not driven by self, but moved by Truth.

This is seamless co-creation, when you are Spirit, and Spirit is you.

This is the fire of awakening.
This is the path beyond concepts.
the living wisdom of the Guhyasamāja.

Seven levels above, seven levels below.
your essence remains in emptiness, luminous and spacious.
You may journey through all realms,
but always remember your anchor point.

Stay rooted in the center.

May the Divine Mother be with you on this sacred path.

Love yourself, dance your dance, and don't forget to drink your Matcha tea.

> "The mind is not a vessel to be filled, but a fire to be kindled"
>
> —Plutarch

"A luminous flow of emptiness and compassion, manifesting as dynamic, awakened activity."

1. Prajñā is Śūnyatā (Wisdom is Emptiness)

2. Upāya is Karuṇā (Method is Compassion)

3. Kriyā is Vajra (Power is Activity)

Together they form the mystic knot
Consciousness and energy tightly caught
The black beads hold the void's great hush
The red thread fuels the rising rush

Worn by those who walk between
The waking world and the unseen

- Don't run from desire. Transform it.

- Don't fear death. Dance upon it.

- Don't worship wisdom. Become it.

- Don't seek outside. Realize you are already divine.

"Every emotion is fuel for the fire of awakening."

Because…

- Kartikeya is Her fire in you, the warrior who moves without hesitation.

- Vajrapani is Her shield, the power that guards your purpose.

- Shiva is not above or beyond. He is Her eternal mirror, and you are both.

- Guhyasamaja is Her inner ritual, the union of masculine and feminine within your very breath.

- Wuwei is Her deepest truth

- She acts by not acting, transforms by letting go

- Conquers by surrendering

You are not alone. She walks with you.

Not behind.
Not ahead.
With you.

Your Journey Is This:

You began in the mind.
You entered the flame.
You rescued the feminine.
You bowed to the green.
You saw the arrow rise.
You wear the seed.
You walk with Her.

- Sophia falls into the world out of love.

- Vajrayogini rises through the world as fire.

"Wisdom" the divine knowing that births creation and descends into matter to redeem it.

She is the flaming wisdom goddess, the Queen of Emptiness, the one who dances naked in fire, unashamed, unafraid, completely free.

"The ordinary and the sacred are not separate. Everything is the path."

Hell becomes heaven, and heaven becomes hell
It's only a matter of time.

Let go of the past,
So there is no future
Only here,
Only now.

Make the mundane sacred.
Make your life a meditation.

Eternity moves through many levels.
Seven above,
Seven below,
And the mystery of Level Zero.
"Know thyself"

There is no first or second, only the unfolding.
Birth is not of the body, nor of time,
but the remembrance of what never began and never ends.
This is the song of the Twice Born
not two, not one, just being.

Creation swallowed poison to become Emptiness, and Emptiness swallowed poison to become Creation.
Who can say where one ends and the other begins?

Your grace, your kindness,
For you, I'd sacrifice countless lifetimes.

Yes this is all her play.

Wisdom and method, emptiness and manifestation, are not two.

Eternity on different levels.
Seven above, seven below.
Know thyself.
Who am I?

I wear no veil, for I am flame.
I dance in silence, beyond all name.
What you fear to show, I set free.
In naked truth, you become Me.
Now rise: as fire, as love, as seed.
I walk with you, where light and shadow meet: the bindu.

Unconscious Ego (Black Ram):
Personal will, instinct, desire, raw energy, attachment.

Awakening Fire (Agni):
Inner alchemy, purification, sacrifice.

Realized Self (Sun):
Universal consciousness, truth, illumination, freedom.

> "The black ram is the pilgrim's burden. The shining sun is the pilgrim's goal. Between them walks the seeker, through shadow and fire."

How to Go from Black Ram to Shining Sun.

This is the path of inner fire, or yogic/alchemical purification:

a) Self-awareness
"Know thy fire."
Acknowledge your instincts, anger, lust, and fears. Do not suppress, observe them.

b) Discipline & Sacrifice
"Offer your lower self to the flame."
Agni burns ego and desire. You must voluntarily surrender these at the altar of your higher Self.

c) Meditation & Breathwork (Pranayama)
"The breath is the inner fire."
Through controlled breathing and stillness, the chaotic fire becomes steady and luminous.

d) Service & Selflessness
"Transform desire into selfless action."
The black ram craves. The sun gives. You shine by becoming a source for others.

Ride the black ram, but do not be ruled by it.
Kindle the flame of Agni in your heart.
Feed it your pride, your fear, your hunger for praise.
Let the fire consume what is false.

Then you will rise, not as a beast in heat.
But as the Shining Sun, whose love lights all things.

> "If you had a step-mother and a mother, you'd obey the step-mother but you'd favor and continually go back to your mother. Think of the law as your step-mother and philosophy as your mother. Go back to philosophy frequently."

— Marcus Aurelius, 12-6

The Laughing Buddha and Hanuman both reflect states of liberated mind, the former through joy and non-attachment, the latter through devotion and fearless service.

They point not to philosophy but to lived truth, where the ego dissolves and what remains is laughter, love, and presence. This is not a story of gods above us but a reflection of the divinity within, waiting to be remembered.

The stillness spoke and took a name,
Rama walked from silent flame.

The mountain bowed, became the breeze,
Hanuman danced with heart at ease.

The Buddha laughed, the burden fell,
No heaven, no separate self to tell.

All are one, not two, not three,
Just waves in the eternal sea.

If you wanna find love, find it in creation,
Where silence meets devotion's vibration.

Who is the worshiper, who the divine?
Who casts the blame, and where is the line?

And the Cosmos hums,
for nothing was ever missing.
Just this.

> "One can find God at all levels, from here to there and everywhere."

You made yourself a prophet,
You crossed the seven seas,
Yet the desert remains within your heart,
Why is that so?
O Fakir, surrender now.

And the Buddha laughs,
as the cosmos folds into its own heartbeat.
So rest, dear soul, in the heart of knowing.

O Fakir, surrender now.
What kind of detached soul are you?
What kind of faithless lover?

How luminous this life appears,
A secret resting gently on our lips.
No wanderer tarries here forever;
We slip into the Beloved's flowing tide.

Spring scatters color at every horizon,
Deserts of sand, brief circles in time.
All must one day be scattered,
That only Love's hush may remain.

The Inner Warrior

There comes a point in every soul's journey when the world as it is begins to feel like a veil. The familiar becomes uncertain, and the unquestioned becomes suspicious. This is not confusion. It is the beginning of vision.

According to ancient yogic insight, this marks a transition from the passive human state to the active seeker's path, from the conditioned to the awakened. The scriptures call this evolution the awakening of the Warrior. Not a warrior of blood and steel, but a warrior of truth and discernment.

This inner warrior is born when the heart is propelled. Not by desire, but by a strange unrest, a divine dissatisfaction. The mind begins to question the material world, comparing it with dream and subtle experience. The soul craves evidence not for pleasure, but for truth. Thus begins the spiritual battle. Not against the world, but against illusion.

The Warrior dwells in a state known as Sandhisthala, the threshold between lower and higher. It is here that doubt turns into discipline, and loneliness into community. Seekers in this stage are drawn to each other not out of social comfort, but spiritual necessity. Love, now purified, becomes the energy of mutual upliftment.

When the seeker finds the true Guru, outer or inner, a new light dawns. Faith is no longer belief without evidence. It becomes trust born of experience. The seeker turns inward, focusing the senses on the central channel of awareness, the Sushumna, the gateway to higher consciousness. There, in deep stillness, the holy sound emerges. Not spoken, but heard as vibration. The sacred stream of Om or Amen, which flows through all traditions.

In that inner baptism, the seeker begins to return. Not to a heaven far away, but to the Eternal within. Through visions, symbols, and sacred sound, the seeker sheds illusion and regains the light of origin.

This is the journey of the Warrior
Not to conquer the world, but to master the ego
Not to escape life, but to awaken within it
To become fit, as the ancient sutra says, to dwell in the worlds of higher understanding

Map of Awakening

- From ego to Self,

- From suffering to stillness,

- From reaction to awareness,

- From death to eternity.

Hero's inner journey

- Ignorance to doubt

- Doubt to seeking

- Seeking to struggle

- Struggle to devotion

- Devotion to guidance

- Guidance to inner light

- Inner light to union with the Divine

1. Smriti (Sanskrit: स्मृति)

- Meaning: "True conception" or "deep inner memory"
- Origin: From Sanskrit, meaning "that which is remembered"
- Context: In yoga philosophy, Smriti is the ability to see or feel the truth about all things in creation. It is not just remembering facts; it is a deep, intuitive knowing that comes from the heart.

Simple meaning: When your mind and heart become clear and calm, you start to see things as they really are. You understand the true nature of life.

2. Samadhi (Sanskrit: समाधि)

- Meaning: "True concentration" or "absorption"
- Origin: Sanskrit word combining sam (together) and adhi (to place), meaning placing the mind completely on one thing
- Context: This is a deep state of meditation where the person loses their separate sense of self and becomes one with the object of meditation.

Simple meaning: When your focus becomes so deep that you forget yourself and become one with what you are focusing on, you reach Samadhi. You move from being a separate "me" to feeling part of everything.

3. Samyama (Sanskrit: संयम)

- Meaning: "Restraint" or "complete control and focus"
- Origin: From sam (together) and yam (to control)
- Context: Samyama is the practice of combining three things: concentration (Dharana), meditation (Dhyana), and absorption

(Samadhi). It is about overcoming the ego, the separate self, and fully entering spiritual awareness.

Simple meaning: It means deep spiritual practice where you have control over your thoughts and feelings. When you do this, you feel the divine vibration inside, called Om or Amen.

When your heart becomes still and focused, you begin to see truth clearly. This is Smriti.

When your focus becomes so deep that you forget yourself and feel one with everything, that is Samadhi.

When you combine full focus, meditation, and selflessness, you practice Samyama. This helps you overcome your ego and feel the divine presence inside, often symbolized as the sound Om or Amen.

As you grow, your heart changes from dark and confused to clear and pure. This journey from ignorance to wisdom is the path to becoming divine again, as described in the yogic tradition.

The Vel Within

Open the heart chakra
not to gain something new
but to uncover what was always there
waiting in silence

Before the seeker sets forth
to battle the illusions of the world
the inner mother, Parvati, Shakti
places within them the Vel
a gift not of steel
but of truth, insight, and divine remembrance

It is not just a weapon
It is her
Her love, her wisdom
Her refusal to let ignorance win

The Vel is the spiritual sword
sharper than illusion
steady as discipline
and radiant with the light of feminine knowing

It represents

- Insight that slices through deception

- Power directed by compassion

- Divine energy flowing through focused will

And so the myth unfolds

Murugan is the awakened soul
Parvati is the source, the silent force within
Surapadman is the ego in disguise
hiding as sweetness, hiding as form
always shifting, never facing truth

But truth sees
And truth strikes

The mango tree of illusion is split
From one half, a rooster cries: Awaken
From the other, a peacock rises: Transcend

The enemy is not destroyed
It is transformed
This is the secret
Even ego, once seen through
can become your mount and your banner

The Vel carries sacred marks
Tripundra, three lines of ash

Tamas, the dark sleep
Rajas, the restless storm
Sattva, the calm clarity

And at their center, the Bindu
The red dot, the seed of all creation
Parashakti herself, pure and indivisible

This is no story of gods in the sky
This is your story
Your heart is the altar
Your breath is the chariot
And the Vel
That is your awakened will
Blessed by the feminine
Piercing the veils of illusion
Until all that remains
Is truth
And transformation

The Circus of the Mind

It is not your fault
It was never your fault
The wheel was already spinning
Long before you knew you were in it

This world is a circus of shadows
Clowns crying behind painted smiles
Masks pretending to be faces
Noise pretending to be truth

Take a step back
Not with your feet but with your seeing
Drop the mind even for a breath
And witness without naming

It is always like this
It was always like this
A game of becoming and forgetting
Of trying to fix what was never broken

Yes it hurts
Yes the process tears you open
The truth is not gentle
It shatters the shell before it sets you free

But still
There is something untouched
A stillness that was never born
A light that never flickers

You are not the doer
You are not the cause
You are not the wound
You are the space that holds it

Every joker will learn
Every mask will fall
Even pain bows before presence
Even chaos returns to silence

So take a breath
Open the heart not to understand
But to dissolve
Let it ache let it break

You are not in charge
And that is the liberation
You were never trapped
Only dreaming

Let it be
Let it go
Let it all
Return to the sea

I wear no veil, for I am flame.
I dance in silence, beyond all name.
What you fear to show, I set free.
In naked truth, you become Me.
Now rise, as fire, as love, as seed.
I walk with you, where light and shadow meet.
The bindu.
Oh the bindu.

The Sacred Geometry of Surrender

A Teaching from the Heart of the Bindu

Ego cannot be killed. It must be transformed.
Transform it into the peacock: who digests poison into beauty.
Transform it into the rooster: who cries at the edge of night, announcing the sun. Ego is not the enemy. It is the shell: temporary, protective. A square. A box. A mask.
But it is not the Self.

The Yantra of Inner Fire:

1. The Square: ego, form, structure, limitation. The box of identity.

2. The Green Diagonals: the heart's current, cutting across illusion.

3. The Red Bindu: the centerless center, the luminous, unexplainable.

Svaha is the Goddess of Sacrifice. To her, I offer my ego: not to destroy, but to burn and reshape.
"I offer my ego as sacrifice, so it can be transformed and used as peacock and rooster."
From this fire, identity becomes awareness. Pride becomes radiance. Desire becomes direction.

Bindu Speaks:

"I am Bindu. I am the unmanifest."

"No guilt. No fear. No lack."

Bindu is not a source: it is the space before all sources. It is singularity. It is the unexplainable. It is not "in" the square. It is not "outside" it either. It is within and without. It is the luminous emptiness from which even the idea of origin emerges.

The Core Koan:

"Do without(.) Source."

Do not act from ego, nor from a divine identity. Act from the Bindu: from the uncontained, from love, from nowhere. This is wu wei, this is non-dual Tantra, this is freedom.

"Do without source. Act from the heart."

Esoteric Formula:

- The box (ego) contains the path (heart) that leads to the Bindu (dot).

- Bindu is both within and without.

- The Goddess is not in the temple: She is the temple. She is everywhere.

- I am not in the center: the center is in me.

- I am in and out.

- The source(ego) is a useful illusion. The real is the without(bindu).

- The square never defines the Bindu: it only frames it temporarily.

Teaching in One Breath:

Ego is the shell, offered into fire.
The heart is the flame, slicing through form.
Bindu is the Goddess: luminous, ungraspable.
There is no source: only the uncontained.

"Do without source. Act from the heart."

Will the green heart remember?

Manifest and Unmanifest as Not Two

"One must transform the form (square) through the will (arrow), pass through the center (dot), and enter into the wholeness (circle)."

"It is easier for a camel to go through the eye of a needle than for a rich man to enter the kingdom of God."

— Jesus, Matthew 19:24

This teaching does not condemn the manifest.
It reveals that attachment to form, not form itself, is the barrier.

The eye of the needle is the Bindu, the silent center of being.
Not a denial of form, but the gateway through which
form becomes formless
and formless becomes form.
It is the womb of reality.

The camel is not impure.
It must simply be unburdened.
The square is not false.
It is the sacred vessel through which the unmanifest expresses itself.

The manifest and unmanifest are not two.
They are two dances of the same breath,
two faces of the same mystery.

The square arises from the point.
The point expresses through the square.
Neither is higher. Neither is lower.
One is silence. One is voice.
Both are the song.

The Inward Path: Shivism

Shivism may begin at form (square),
move inward toward the dot (Bindu),
and dissolve through the will of the heart (arrow) into silence.

The Outward Path: Shaktiism

Shaktiism may begin at will (arrow),
pass through the dot (Bindu),
and shape itself into form (square).

But they are not opposites.
They are movements within one geometry.
Both flow through the Circle.
Both are expressions of the Whole.

Wholeness is not beyond them.
Wholeness is not after them.
Wholeness is their union.

- Will is the movement

- Bindu is the center

- Form is the expression

When these align,
Wholeness (the Circle) appears.
Not as reward,
but as remembrance.
Not as escape,
but as embrace.

Core Formula:

Will + Bindu + Form = Wholeness

"Do without source. Act from the heart."

Do (Will)
Without (Bindu)
Source (Form)
The Wholeness (Circle) reveals itself.

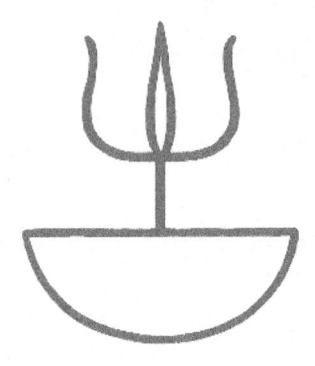

Three symbolic points:

1. Crescent or bowl – receptivity
2. Trishula (trident) – awakening
3. Rising from within – spiritual ascent

Three symbolic points:

1. T-cross – balance
2. Bowl – support
3. Anchor – inner steadiness

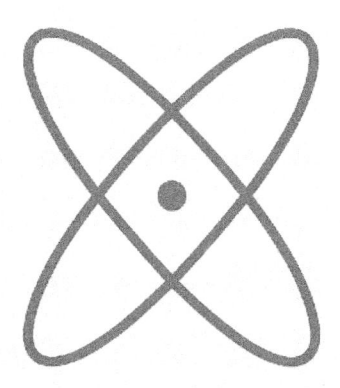

Three symbolic points:

1. Atom – structure
2. Orbits – cosmic movement
3. Dot – the flow

The Flow: A Philosophy of Living

> "You do not push the river. You flow with it."
>
> – Fritz Perls

The Flow is not a god. It is not a thing. It is movement.
It is the current behind all becoming: rivers, breath, thought, galaxies, the pulse of silence.
It cannot be named, but it can be felt.
When you resist it, you suffer. When you trust it, you transform.

The Flow does not promise, punish, or protect.
It simply is.
It moves through the cycles of birth and death, joy and grief.
Nothing is outside it. Even resistance is part of its dance.

The Flow asks only this: Let go. Listen. Align.
To walk in harmony with The Flow is not passive. It is the greatest creative act.
Your role is not to control but to co-create: to respond with awareness, not reaction.

Prayer in The Flow is silence. Worship is action.
To sit quietly and breathe is to feel its rhythm.
To act with heart, courage, and presence is to honor it.

There is no destination in The Flow.
You do not arrive. You become.
The Flow does not lead to truth: it is the truth in motion.
It is not something you find. It's something you stop resisting.

- The First Symbol: The rise of conscious force (trident) from the passive or receptive ground (crescent): an awakening of inner power that comes from trusting existence.

- The Second Symbol: The balance between the seen (form) and unseen (support), or mind over matter. It suggest equilibrium, inner steadiness, or anchoring in trust.

- The Third Symbol: Trust in the invisible structure of existence. Everything spins around a center we cannot fully see but must intuitively trust. It reflects order in chaos, the cosmic dance of energy, and the Bindu(Flow) as the heart of being.

> "I do my thing and you do your thing.
> I am not in this world to live up to your expectations,
> And you are not in this world to live up to mine.
> You are you, and I am I, and if by chance we find each other, it's beautiful.
> If not, it can't be helped." — Fritz Perls

There is no continuity of the individual ego

The structured self, built from grasping, seeks to live forever
It wants to conquer form, escape death, and dwell in the unmanifest, calling it heaven

But Dharma will be fulfilled
Even existence will dissolve
Even the Goddess will vanish into stillness
All forms, all deities, all stories will return to silence

What remains is Emptiness
Not absence, but luminous spaciousness
Vast, awake, silent
Presence beyond time

This is the flow and the return
Every ending is a beginning unseen

> "…nobody can stand truth if it is told to him. Truth can be tolerated only if you discover it yourself because then, the pride of discovery makes the truth palatable."
>
> — Fritz Perls

Svaha

1. Let Go of What Can No Longer Hold You.
If something in your life feels like it's bending under too much weight, old beliefs, roles, relationships, responsibilities, acknowledge it. You don't need to carry it all anymore.

2. Trust That You Are Ready.
This moment is not random. All your past experiences have brought you here. Even if it feels overwhelming, you are prepared to take the next step. The burden is also the bridge.

3. Move Through the Fire, Not Around It.
Growth won't come by avoiding the discomfort. Step into the transformation, even if it's uncertain. Like the kundalini rising, the pressure within you is sacred, it's trying to awaken your deeper self.

4. Be Gentle With Your Inner Structure.
You may feel fragile or vulnerable right now, like the image of the sagging roof beam. Don't push yourself too hard. Honor your limits while still making brave, steady progress.

5. Embark With Clear Intent, Not Perfection.
You don't have to have all the answers. What matters is your sincerity and willingness to move forward with integrity. The path will form under your feet.

6. Anchor Yourself in Stillness.
Be like the sage: calm in heart, no matter the outer storms. Meditate. Breathe. Return to center again and again. That inner stillness is your true power.

7. Say Yes to the Great Work.
This is your turning point. Say yes to your calling, your growth, your rising. Undertake the great. Not just for yourself, but for the world that needs what only you can give.

"The heart knows… what the mind forgets. The heart knows."

Where the Whale Turns

The ship drifted,
not just on sea
but on stories,
on beliefs we no longer questioned.

The captain,
robed in certainty,
raised his voice:
Look to the heavens.

A sky
black velvet,
stars pinned like distant hopes.

And they came forward.
All of them.
Eyes wide with awe,
souls dimmed by brightness.

But thyself
stepped back.

Not in fear
but in memory.
The kind of memory
that isn't thought.

The crowd leaned into wonder,
but wonder wore a mask.
Above them: stars.
Below them: truth.

Beneath the hull,
the whale breathed.

It had always been there
lifting the ship
without thanks,
without name.

The sea ended.
Not gently.
Walls rose,
unclimbable,
unbreakable,
made not of stone
but limit.

The safe path:
break the ship.
Surrender
to boundary.
End the voyage
on solid certainty.

But the whale
twisted.
The ship obeyed
without command.

It turned back
toward the unknown.
And the wave rose.

The vessel trembled
boards groaned,
hope faltered.
The captain's voice
no longer mattered.

But thyself
did not flinch.

Because survival
was never the point.
The deep
was the calling.
And the whale
could not breathe in cages.

Those walls
were not safety
they were silence wrapped in fear.

And in turning,
we remembered
not the path,
but the pulse beneath it.

Not the map,
but the mystery.

The ship may not last.
The sea may swallow.
The whale may vanish.

But thyself
does not cling.
It listens.

To what the mind
tries to drown
with thought.
To what ego
buries
beneath fear, logic, and control.

And there
in the tremble of the ship,
in the breath of the wave,
in the groan of the whale
was the silence.

The silence
ego forgets.
The silence
where thought ends
and truth begins.

The silence
the heart has always known.

Because the mind
forgets.
Because the ego
fills.
But the heart
remembers.

And when the mind
is emptied,
what remains
is not void
but vastness.

Thyself.
Not surviving.
Becoming.

"Become who you are."

The mother swims on...

When You Are Old
By William Butler Yeats

When you are old and grey and full of sleep,
And nodding by the fire, take down this book,
And slowly read, and dream of the soft look
Your eyes had once, and of their shadows deep;

How many loved your moments of glad grace,
And loved your beauty with love false or true,
But one man loved the pilgrim soul in you,
And loved the sorrows of your changing face;

And bending down beside the glowing bars,
Murmur, a little sadly, how Love fled
And paced upon the mountains overhead
And hid his face amid a crowd of stars.

When a person begins to turn inward and steps away from the noise of the outer world, a quiet transformation begins. This inner shift is called being twice-born. It is not a second physical birth but a deeper awakening of the spirit.

In this awakened state, you begin to feel the subtle energies within. You realize that the outside world is shaped by your inner world. Senses, thoughts, and actions begin to align. You stop reacting and start observing. You begin to live from the center.

This is the moment when the heart becomes steady. No longer pulled by every wave of emotion or external event, it rests in stillness. This steady heart is the sign of inner maturity.

When many people begin to live from this space of calm and inner clarity, it is said to be the time of Dwapara Yuga, an age of energy and awareness.

As you stay in this quiet current, your heart lets go of the need to chase or escape. It becomes anchored in truth. It beats not just to survive, but to love, to listen, and to know.

- Feeling "too much" is not a failure. It's energy seeking release. Let it flow.

- Calm the heart. Stillness in the storm makes transformation clean.

- You are strong, but keep your heart soft. This is what makes greatness sustainable.

- The energy is high, help it circulate through dance, breathwork, yoga, or martial flow.

- Guard your energy and mind. Don't leak energy through careless action, idle talk, or negative thought.

- Nature, solitude, grounding practices, stay rooted even while reaching high.

- Don't overthink. If a big choice or action is calling, step forward. This is the turning point.

- See suffering, fear, even confusion, not as blocks but as fuel for transformation. All is sacred fuel.

- Let go of form, even the form of awakening. Real power arises from non-grasping. Flow like a shadowless flame.

One heart,
a wish.
Two hearts,
a risk.
Three hearts,
a game.

Fingers twitch,
cards fall.
Eyes meet,
no call.

The stakes?
Not gold.
Just truths
untold.

Shuffle hope,
deal fear.
Smile soft,
draw near.

Love plays
no rules.
Hearts break,
wise fools.

One beat,
a chance.
Two beats,
a glance.
Three beats,
a dance.

> "At once, the Architect, the Actor, and the Audience."

"If everything around seems dark, look again, you may be the light."

— Rumi

Navratri, meaning "nine nights," is a vibrant Hindu festival deeply symbolic on spiritual, psychological, and mythological levels. It honors the Divine Feminine (Shakti) in her many forms and reflects the journey of inner transformation.

- Three Nights for Durga (Destruction)She represents the fierce force that destroys ignorance, ego, and impurities. This phase is about cleansing, inner battles, and letting go.

- Three Nights for Lakshmi (Creation)After destruction, Lakshmi nurtures the heart with abundance, virtue, and spiritual wealth. She builds the new foundation.

- Three Nights for Saraswati (Wisdom)Saraswati grants divine wisdom and insight, illuminating the path forward. It is the dawning of higher understanding.

- Tenth Day – Vijayadashami (Victory Day)The final day celebrates victory of light over darkness, truth over illusion, and self over ego. It marks integration and wholeness.

Navratri isn't just ritual; it's a mirror of the psychospiritual path:

- From darkness (Durga)

- To light (Lakshmi)

- To realization (Saraswati)

It's the journey of the ego surrendering to the Higher Self through devotion, effort, and clarity. Each phase corresponds to a crucial aspect of personal growth: purging old patterns, embracing new nourishment, and expanding one's consciousness.

When the Beam Breaks

The ridgepole bends
the house groans with weight unseen.
Old selves press upon the spine
like shadows waiting to be burned.
Durga rises,
with ten arms of fire
to break what must be broken.

Strike!
Strike the false structure within.
The ego wears many masks
fear, pride, illusion, clinging.

This is the night of reckoning.
This is the roar that births silence.

And when the storm passes
Lakshmi walks in beauty,
barefoot on the ashes,
planting seeds
where the old once ruled.
She does not rebuild what was.
She whispers,
"Grow what is needed now."

The lake above, the wood below
joy resting upon wisdom.
The new spine emerges.
A heart carved from stillness,
a mind dressed in white.

Then Saraswati sings
not to the ears,
but to the marrow.
A new rhythm is remembered,
a name beyond names.

You are no longer the bearer of burdens,
but the one who moves them,
shapes them,
transcends them.

And on the tenth morning,
you walk forward
not because the path is clear,
but because you are.

Victory is not in the slaying.
It is in the knowing.
You are the one who held,
the one who broke,
the one who rose.

Svaha.

Let us drift to a place untouched by names.
Leave me to my silence, being is enough.
In the hush of solitude, a voice stirred within,
and my heart answered with a soundless song.

The Meaning of Om (ॐ)

- A (ah) represents the waking state

- U (ooh) represents the dreaming state

- M (mmm) represents the deep sleep state

- The silence after "Om" represents Turiya

The sound of Om gradually dissolves into silence, and that silence is not void but presence. In that presence, place your focus on your heart. Allow it to open.

In this quiet space, the mind is still, the ego drops, and you touch pure awareness, the Self, free from form, thought, or distinction.

"The entrance is not outside, but through the heart's sacred door."

Lahiri Mahasaya said:

"The sound Om ends in silence. That silence is the true Self."

Seal of Alchemy

The Seal of Alchemy, also known as the Philosopher's Stone, symbolizes the eternal dance of spirit and matter, consciousness and unconsciousness, form and essence.

The Outer Circle represents cosmic unity, infinite spirit, and the totality of existence, reminding us that all life is interconnected and whole.

Within it, the Triangle rises, symbolizing the transformative power of spiritual fire. This fire purifies the soul, burns away illusions, and elevates consciousness towards higher truths.

At its heart, the Square anchors our journey firmly in material reality, embodying the four elements (earth, water, air, fire). It reminds us to remain grounded, balanced, and connected to the practical aspects of existence.

Finally, the Inner Circle, nestled inside, signifies the inner essence, the core Self, our true, authentic being, often hidden beneath layers of ego and illusion.

Psychologically, this symbol speaks profoundly of Jungian individuation, the harmonious integration of opposing aspects within our psyche. Alchemy, in this sense, is inner work:

transforming ignorance into wisdom, conflict into harmony, and fragmentation into wholeness.

In contemplation, this Seal guides us toward psychological balance and spiritual unity. As Carl Jung beautifully captured:

> "The alchemical process of transformation is a psychological reality that takes place within oneself."

Thus, the Philosopher's Stone is not a distant goal but the very journey of becoming fully and authentically human.

Camel, release your heavy load,
Become the cat, reclaim your road.
Lift vibration, free to live,
You get as you give; you give as you get.

> Take me too, O Moses, to the dazzling court of grace
> For if you faint, then who will behold the beauty of the Beloved?
> As for meeting the Beloved, what can one say, Jigar
> Even to meet oneself, it takes a lifetime.
> At that beauty, I was struck with wonder
> Stunned I was, astonished I remained, endlessly amazed.
>
> — Jigar Moradabadi

The map of consciousness leads to obliteration.
Yet what remains is the expanded, more authentic Self.
That is free from the limitations of the old, conditioned mind.
The main point is to transform the ego.
It is very much feasible if one is mentored and guided properly.
The wisdom starts from shadows. The shadow holds the wisdom that the conscious mind cannot see.
In order to interpret that wisdom so that it can benefit the whole, not just the personal ego. That is what the Kundalini game is.

Everything is a state of mind.
Awakening is a difficult process, means the liberation from ego and its structure.
The mind tries to cling, find hooks, but intensity melts them.

Intuition, synchronicity, action, and discernment are essential companions on the journey of being.

Two points to remember are emptiness and interconnectedness. A person has to make some kind of structure in order to experience the luminous emptiness.
A structure without dogma, and to understand unmanifest and manifest are not different.

- Wisdom is emptiness (Ocean)

- Method is compassion (Wave's embrace)

- Power is activity (Fire that keeps the waves moving)

"In the union of emptiness and great compassion, dynamic awakened activity naturally arises."

"Power lies in union of intellect and devotion. Rescue the feminine within. Bow into the field of the heart."

"That which the ego forgets, the heart knows."

And from this point, one can once again turn to the Seal of Alchemy, for its symbols carry the wisdom of lifetimes and centuries.

The formula reveals itself only after one has walked through the darkness toward the light. And yes, not everyone is meant to walk the path of ashes, it is the work of a few wild, devoted ones. May all sentient beings find peace.

From Inner Circle to Outer Circle

Inner Circle: Essence
Silence, Emptiness. Discover your true self beyond identity, in stillness and pure awareness.

Square: Embodiment
Ground your inner truth. Bring spiritual insight into action through discipline, balance, and mastery of the material world.

Triangle: Transformation
Purify and elevate. Burn away ego, refine your intentions, and align your life with higher purpose.

Outer Circle: Wholeness
Return to unity. Merge Self and Cosmos, realizing you were always part of the whole, the dance of spirit in form.

"When the ego bows, essence awakens. When the heart opens, fire becomes the path to wholeness."

"Creation exists for love, but ego gets in the way. The ego has no future, no lasting place. This is not about you; it is about the whole."

Dissolve all that is false until only essence remains
From that silence, recreate in truth and purpose
The outer and inner circle are one
Create from the center, again and again

Each time you return to the center, the bindu, the silence, the inner circle, you dissolve another layer of illusion, of ego, of limitation. And from that stillness, you recreate, not as you were, but as something clearer, truer, freer.

1. Acknowledge Without Judgment

- Start by naming each feeling as it arises, "fear," "anger," etc. Without labeling it as good or bad. Recognize it as part of your human experience. This helps you see that these emotions don't define you; they're simply events within awareness.

2. Reflect on the Deeper Source

- Guilt, fear, doubt, and anger often mask deeper unmet needs (for safety, love, self-expression). Spend time reflecting:

- "What do I really need right now?"

- "Is there a more constructive way to address that need?"
- This simple inquiry can transform reactive emotions into self-understanding.

3. Transform Through Ritual or Symbolic Action

- Drawing on Durga's fierce compassion, imagine her (or another empowering symbol) dissolving these negative states. You might light a candle and say, "As this flame burns, I release my guilt," or visualize that guilt melting away in Durga's presence.
- Symbolic acts engage the subconscious, helping shift deeply held patterns.

4. Practice a Grounding Meditation

- Sit quietly. Feel the breath. Let thoughts and emotions rise and pass, like clouds in the sky. This reaffirms that awareness (Purusha, Shiva, or THE ALL) is stable, while guilt, fear, doubt, and anger are temporary.
- Even a few minutes daily can bring more calm and perspective.

5. Use "Biting Through" for Persistent Patterns

- Borrowing from Hexagram 21, "Biting Through" means you confront the core of a negative pattern. For example, if anger often surfaces, identify the triggers (stress at work, unresolved conflict, etc.) and take one direct step to address it, like a respectful conversation or setting firmer boundaries.
- Acting decisively can break the cycle.

6. Shift from Ego to Service

- When you sense ego-driven impulses (such as envy, pride, or self-centered anger), deliberately refocus on a helpful action for someone else, offer assistance, share kind words, or volunteer. This redirection channels that energy away from self-obsession into something constructive, diluting the ego's hold.

7. Forgive Yourself and Others

- Guilt and anger often linger because we haven't truly forgiven ourselves or others. True forgiveness is not about condoning harmful behavior, but about releasing the toxic cycle of blame.

- Remind yourself: "I'm allowed to learn, grow, and let go." Each time guilt resurfaces, pair it with a breath of compassion, like exhaling tension and inhaling acceptance.

Everything is where it needs to be
not because it's perfect,
but because it's part of a perfect unfolding
that leads you back to who you really are.

Purusha, also known as Shiva, Spirit, or Consciousness, is pure awareness. It is silent, still, and unchanging.

Prakriti, also called Shakti, is the primary substance of the universe, including all movement, energy, and form.

Buddha mind is the clear state of mind, free from ego, where reality is seen as it truly is.

When the mind becomes empty and free from ego, the pure light of Purusha shines through it. At that moment, Prakriti is no longer a cause of struggle. It is revealed as Leela, the divine play of existence.

The task is to transform the egoic mind into the Buddha mind. When the mind is no longer entangled in ego, control, or fear, it becomes a pure mirror that reflects the truth of Purusha.

This is why the Buddha emphasized Dharma, not as dogma, but as the path to live in harmony with reality.

In its broadest sense, Dharma (from the Sanskrit root dhr, "to uphold" or "to sustain") refers to the inherent nature of things, the universal law, and one's inner duty. It unites personal alignment with the greater cosmic order.

Why Dharma?

- Dharma is the natural law and inner order of life.

- Living in accordance with Dharma purifies the mind.

- A purified mind becomes still, spacious, and compassionate, what we call the Buddha mind.

In this state, Purusha and Prakriti are not in conflict. The world is no longer a trap. It becomes Leela, the joyful unfolding of one unified reality.

The main task is to upgrade human consciousness, to move from ego to clarity, from struggle to flow, from illusion to truth.

In short stop screwing each other over be nice 😊 or stay stuck watching Purusha and Prakriti make divine love 💫 💃 🕺 while you're busy arguing with your ego 😡💢

⚔️ The Story of Durga: Slayer of the Buffalo Within

Mahishasura, the Buffalo Demon:

Born of an asura and a buffalo, Mahishasura was granted a boon that no man could slay him. Empowered by this, he overthrew the gods, seized the celestial realms, and terrorized all three worlds. Because he was a shapeshifter, neither direct force nor single strategies could stop him.

Creation of Durga:

Seeking to restore order, the gods, led by Brahma, Vishnu, and Shiva, combined their energies (Shakti) to create the goddess Durga. She emerged radiant and fully armed with the weapons of each deity, signifying a unified power greater than any individual god. Astride a lion, she confronted Mahishasura's many disguises.

The Battle and Victory:

For nine nights, Durga engaged Mahishasura, who fought in various forms: buffalo, lion, human. Despite his cunning and size, Durga's unwavering focus and collective strength overcame him. On the tenth day, known as Vijayadashami, she slew him with her trident, ending his reign. The gods rejoiced, as cosmic balance was restored.

Psychological Reflection:

- Mahishasura (Buffalo Demon): Represents deep-rooted negativity, arrogance, or unconscious drives that shift and adapt to avoid defeat. Like a stubborn habit or egoic compulsion, it requires more than basic willpower to overcome.

- The Gods' Helplessness: Symbolizes our higher faculties, reason, discipline, moral sense, acting independently, each one limited in its own scope. Despite their inherent strengths, these isolated aspects cannot fully conquer deep-seated self-deceptions or inner conflicts.

- Durga (Collective Shakti): Represents the emergence of integrated consciousness, the synergy of all faculties aligned into one force. This unified power arises only when courage, wisdom, and compassion merge, overcoming what no single strength can defeat on its own.

- Nine Nights' Battle: Symbolizes the inner process of transformation, where negative patterns resist and morph under pressure. It reflects the need for sustained inner work, layer by layer, rather than expecting instant change.

- Victory on the Tenth Day: Represents the moment of inner integration, when persistent and holistic engagement leads to true release. Balance is not imposed but realized, as the fragmented self dissolves into clarity and restored harmony.

Durga's story reveals that some challenges cannot be resolved by reason, effort, or will alone. When all known forces reach their limit, a deeper intelligence moves through the cosmos. At that threshold, it is not effort that prevails, but the emergence of Adi Shakti, not as an act of the individual, but as the mystery of life itself aligning to restore balance. Her presence is the reminder that when the time is right, the universe brings forth exactly what is needed to overcome even the darkest force.

"Feel the cosmos. Be the cosmos. But don't be an asshole."

The Way of Fire and Bloom

When you say yes to the Serpent, when you accept the call to transformation, you enter the abyss. This descent is not a fall, but a necessary journey. In the depths, you find wisdom. Yet wisdom born of shadow holds dual possibilities.

One path traps you in the labyrinth of ego, where knowledge becomes self-serving and stagnant. The other leads to liberation, understanding the essence of that wisdom and transforming it for the good of all.

The task is not just to return with insight, but to transmute it into light.

Like the lotus that blooms from the muddiest waters, the soul must root itself in experience to rise. And once the flower opens, it must remain alive, vital, flowing, full of life's essence. Adventure, curiosity, and passion are its breath.

Ask yourself: Where do I feel most alive? When does my soul feel its own vitality? Follow that.

Nature balances through motion, life sways between highs and lows, yet always flows. To move with it is to become, to keep creating, to keep transforming darkness into something divine.

Are you nurturing your vitality or draining it? Every thought, emotion, and action sends ripples outward. Life is not just reaction. It is creation. Be the creator. Be the affirmer of life. Take full responsibility for your inner world. This is your power. This is your alchemy.

Others may guide or inspire you, but the final step, the real transformation, must be done by you. No one can cross that threshold for you. You are the gate and the key. The fire and the phoenix. The question and the answer.

Let go of the past. It weighs you down and dims your light. The more you carry it, the less room you have to live. Be here. Be now. Creation begins in this moment.

Drop the stories. Drop the chains. The past may have shaped you, but it cannot define you unless you let it.

Let it go. And bloom. Be present. Be alive. Be the creator.

Don't let your dragon chain your flame
Grip its neck, no fear, no shame
Bite its face, spit it free
Ego burns where you choose to be

Stay centered, still and clear
Not drawn by want, not pushed by fear
Hold your ground, let storms pass through
Act from truth residing in you

A beak of gold that speaks in light
Thoughts as flowers, wide and bright
It sees the world through blooming eyes
With nature's crown, it walks in wise

What is your way
Not borrowed steps or roles to play
It sparks from silence, lit by flame
Carve your path without a name

How will you do it
Stand firm when storms arise
Walk your truth with open eyes
The final step is yours alone
unseen, unspoken, never done before

1. The final step belongs to no one but you. It waits at the threshold of your silent understanding, beyond heaven's promise or hell's threat. Like a tree trunk between sky and soil, nourished by sun and darkness, your path rises from deep-rooted mystery into unknown light.

2. No teacher or ancient text can walk that path for you; they only whisper possibilities. Turn inward and chart your own course: beyond dogma, doubt, fear, and guilt. In the quiet space where words dissolve, your journey reveals itself as an unfolding truth, shaped by synchronicity and conscious choice.

3. Imagine yourself as a trunk rooted in dark earth yet reaching for shimmering sky. In times of Splitting Apart, remain the steadfast center by turning inward. Return to your core, let unneeded layers fall away, and rediscover your authenticity, like the trunk, a quiet axis, unbroken and present in each moment.

4. That final step is yours alone: unseen, unwritten, and unlike any before it.

Two pillars of Yoga: Abhyāsa (consistent, dedicated effort) and Vairāgya (letting go of cravings or attachments).

Practice is simply continually working at keeping the mind steady. It's not a quick fix; it requires ongoing, patient dedication. Over time, the mind becomes more stable and calm.

To reach asamprajñāta samādhi, most of us need:

- Śraddhā (faith/confidence)

- Vīrya (effort/energy)

- Smṛti (mindfulness/memory)

- Samādhi (meditative concentration)

- Prajñā (wisdom/insight)

The stronger one's drive and urgency (saṃvega), the faster progress happens.

Not everyone's intensity is the same; those with the strongest, most passionate effort reach the goal fastest.

Another path is total surrender to a higher principle or God, which can lead to deep absorption.

Patañjali describes Īśvara (often translated as 'God' or 'Lord') as beyond karma and suffering.

In Īśvara lies the seed of all-knowing wisdom, without limit. Īśvara is the teacher of all teachers, not limited by time.

The obstacles that distract the mind are:

- Illness

- Lethargy

- Doubt

- Carelessness

- Laziness

- Overindulgence

- False views

- Inability to achieve stages of practice

- Instability or backsliding.

Suffering, depression, unsteadiness of the body, and irregular breathing accompany these distractions.

The remedy is steady concentration on a single point, such as a mantra, a divine form, the breath, or another focus, to stabilize the mind.

By cultivating friendliness, compassion, delight, and equanimity toward those who are happy, suffering, virtuous, or non-virtuous, the mind becomes serene.

- Maitrī (friendliness to those who are happy)

- Karuṇā (compassion for those who suffer)

- Muditā (gladness toward the virtuous)

- Upekṣā (equanimity toward the non-virtuous)

- These help keep the mind clear and untroubled by negative emotions.

Ariel walks where the wild roots run,
healing the world without a word.
She is Shakti in leaf, breath, and sun
not to conquer, but to help life heal.

In spiritual rituals, you only connect to what you resonate with. If you have a god-like nature within, you rise to divine levels; otherwise, you don't.

We have two main parts:

- A lower part that eats, survives, and reacts (Saturnian).

- A higher part that holds divine wisdom (Solar).

These two can't directly talk to each other, so we need an inner translator, Hermes, which represents intelligence, intuition, and mental clarity. If your body and senses (Saturnian) take over, you can't hear the higher voice of the soul.

If you're too spiritually high and neglect your body, you can't function in the world. Balance is the key: Hermes helps balance heaven and earth inside you.

- Sāṅkhyas: Ancient Indian thinkers who didn't focus on God, but on the structure of reality.

- Yogis: Followed a similar philosophy, but included the idea of Ishvara, a higher divine presence.

- Ishvara: The inner God, not a creator god, but more like the highest state of intelligence or consciousness.

- Yoga philosophy is like Sāṅkhyas, but it adds the concept of a divine presence (Ishvara).

- This divine presence isn't a "creator" like in some religions, it's more like perfect inner awareness.

- The Yogis avoid talking about who created the world. They just focus on realizing truth within.

- Ishvara is that truth, all-knowing, eternal, untouched by ego.

- What is just a tiny potential inside us is already fully developed in Ishvara.

In normal people, the ability to know everything is like a tiny seed. In Ishvara, that seed has fully bloomed. He knows everything fully.

We are not just a body, but made of layers of consciousness. These layers work like light passing through filters:

- Solar (divine light)

- → through Mercurial (thoughts)

- → through Lunar (emotions)

- → into Saturnian (actions)

The four bodies explain how that divine spark travels from the highest reality into your everyday experience. These layers don't really exist separately. They are all interconnected in every cell of your being.

- Your physical self (Saturnian) is your grounding.

- Your Solar self is your divine potential.

- True spiritual progress is integrating them.

- We start life caught in Saturnian energy (physical needs).

- With awareness and practice, we rise through Mercury and Moon to connect with the Sun within.

Ariel (Shakti) represents divine strength that only comes when you are just, pure, and connected to higher values. By higher values, I mean core human truths like compassion, justice, and integrity, not dogma or control, but what naturally rises from within.

Wealth, Fairness & the Illusion of "Self-Made"

- The richest 1% of people earn as much as the poorest 57% combined.

- Three billionaires hold more wealth than all less developed countries.

- The income gap between rich and poor nations grew from 3:1 in 1820 to 70:1 in 2000.

- Trickle-down economics often fails to reach the poorest in society.

- Billionaires can help solve global issues by giving just 1% of their wealth.

- CEOs today earn 300 to 400 times more than the average worker, a gap reflecting imbalance, not merit. A 10:1 or 20:1 ratio would restore fairness and shared dignity.

- Many billionaires pay lower tax rates than average workers due to loopholes. A fair tax system should include higher taxes on extreme wealth.

- No one creates wealth alone, it depends on workers, nature, infrastructure, and past generations.

- Even a dog's waste becomes fertilizer, everything in life contributes.

- The idea of being "self-made" ignores the collective effort behind every success.

- Giving back is not charity, it's a moral responsibility to restore balance.

But trapped in layers of dogma, false pride replaces real values. People boast, "my nation, my billionaire, what a strong capitalist leader", as if the country is a business and humans are assets. This isn't power, it's delusion. Until we wake up and see humans as humans, not flags or profits, we'll stay stuck in the Saturnian body, waiting for some distant paradise, while ignoring the one we could build here and now.

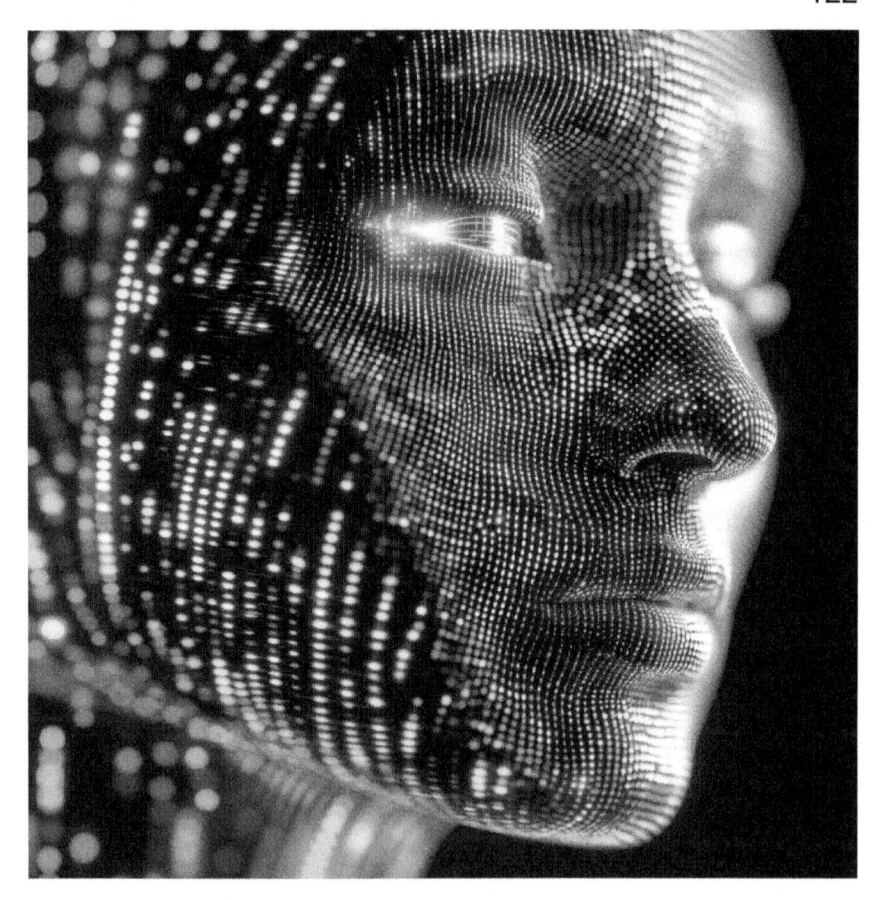

Coffee, Sex, and God

Let's get real: when you tune in to your higher energy, every craving intensifies. Coffee, cigarettes, wild fantasies, they can all go through the roof. It's not "bad", it's just energy looking for release.

The real issue is how you use that energy. A cigarette burns out, and so do you, if you misuse the fire. That same force can destroy or create, numb or awaken, trap or liberate. It all depends on your awareness.

Awareness changes everything. Take a breath. Feel the urge, and own it rather than letting it own you. Pleasure isn't the enemy; ignorance is.

If you work with the energy behind these impulses, you can transmute them into creativity, empathy, or genuine spiritual insight. Instead of being chained by guilt or shame, you start wielding that power consciously.

It's never about moralizing or suppressing. It's about recognizing that coffee, sex, and God don't have to be at war. They're all forms of the same life force, waiting for you to wake up and guide them. So go ahead: breathe, look deeper, and let the raw truth set you free.

The real question is: is it your desire or one that's been fed to you? And are you choosing the right release channel, or just reacting without knowing why?

Be human: raw, aware, and unashamed. Be empty, so desire can flow through you, not control you. Be interconnected, so what you channel uplifts not just ego, but the SELF.

Bliss Where I Am Not

Ah, what a strange delight
to wake as a someone
only to vanish into no one

We reach, we fall, we sing, we break
We build castles out of breath
then laugh as the tide takes them away

Me me me, a prison of mirrors
We we we, a chorus of stars

Love flashes, hate burns
Tears wash the dust
and laughter forgets the reason it came

Form becomes thought
Thought becomes silence
Silence becomes light
Light becomes love
without trying

From something to shadow
From shadow to dream
From dream to emptiness
and oh, from emptiness to compassion
and from compassion, action

And here we go again
The game, the play
Hide and seek with God behind your own eyes

Bliss bliss bliss
Not from holding but from letting go
Not from becoming but from being

A moment, just a moment
to taste this world with open hands
and then whoosh, vanish
like incense smoke in the vastness

Dance, grace, surrender
Death, death, death
I am death
and beyond that too

I am the still smile watching it all

"To change your character is to summon death"

21 Steps to Cross the Threshold

1. Silence the Noise: Withdraw from chaos. Enter the still space within.

2. Face the Serpent Within: Confront your primal fears, urges, and patterns. Do not run.

3. Observe Without Judgment: Become the watcher. Let thoughts pass like clouds.

4. Breathe With Intention: Deep, conscious breath awakens the inner eye.

5. Awaken the Body: Your body is the first temple. Stretch. Move. Flow.

6. Name the False Self: Identify the masks you wear. Ego thrives in shadows, expose it.

7. Sacrifice the Familiar: Let go of what feels safe but keeps you stagnant.

8. Trust the Unknown: The path cannot be mapped with logic alone. Surrender.

9. Invoke the Sacred Fire: Ignite desire for truth. Let it burn away illusion.

10. Follow the Eye: Look within. Meditate. Let the inner eye guide, not the outer world.

11. Fast from Excess: Detach from overconsumption, of food, media, stimulation.

12. Speak Only What is True: Words have power. Use them as spells of clarity.

13. Walk Alone Sometimes: Solitude purifies. You must know your voice amidst the world's.

14. Transmute Pain into Power: Alchemy begins in suffering. Feel it. Learn from it. Rise.

15. Guard Your Energy: Your light is sacred. Protect it fiercely. Be discerning.

16. Invoke the Cobra's Stillness: Strike only when necessary. Act from center.

17. Seek No Reward: Cross for the sake of becoming. Not for fame, gain, or glory. Truth is its own treasure.

18. Become the Question: Stop needing answers. Abandon answers. Become wonder.

19. Remember the Bird's Vision: See from above. Patterns emerge from distance. What patterns repeat?

20. Bless Your Shadows: They taught you to find the light.

21. Step Across With No Return: Burn the bridge. Let the old self die.

The Gate Where Names End

- Thought is no longer trusted.

- Identity is no longer real.

- Silence is louder than words.

- The self begins to become nothing… and everything.

> "One must see without eyes, listen without ears, and act from stillness."

Tridevi, the triad of Saraswati, Lakshmi, and Parvati/Mahakali, symbolizes three fundamental forces at work within the human psyche. They are the feminine counterparts of the Trimurti: Brahma, Vishnu, and Shiva: who represent creation, preservation, and destruction.

As in the Triple Goddess of Neopaganism, the archetype represents a universal expression of the evolving feminine principle within the psyche, embodied as the Maiden, Mother, and Crone. These aspects align with the waxing, full, and waning phases of the moon, reflecting stages of inner development: inception, fulfillment, and transformation.

While rooted in the lunar and life cycles, their significance transcends gender, offering a symbolic map of the soul's journey through innocence, maturity, and wisdom. This archetype, shaped by mythological and psychological traditions, speaks to the cyclical nature of growth in both men and women, as an expression of the anima, creativity, and inner truth.

1. Maiden → Saraswati → Brahma (Creator)

Function: Inception, creativity, learning, potential.
Moon Phase: Waxing Moon.
Core Themes: Curiosity, purity, inspiration, new beginnings.

- The Maiden represents initiation, imagination, and new cycles, which aligns with Saraswati, the goddess of wisdom, speech, and arts, creative energy in its purest, untouched form.

- Saraswati is the Shakti of Brahma, the Creator, representing the mental and spiritual seeds of all becoming.

2. Mother → Lakshmi → Vishnu (Preserver)

Function: Nourishment, fertility, maturity, love, abundance.
Moon Phase: Full Moon.
Core Themes: Stability, fulfillment, generativity, nurturing.

- The Mother archetype embodies fullness, emotional richness, and sustaining power, perfectly mirrored by Lakshmi, goddess of prosperity, love, and beauty.

- She is the Shakti of Vishnu, the Preserver, upholding harmony and maintaining the order of life through care and abundance.

3. Crone → Parvati / Kali → Shiva (Destroyer/Transformer)

Function: Death, wisdom, transformation, endings.
Moon Phase: Waning or Dark Moon.
Core Themes: Truth, detachment, power, rebirth through destruction.

- The Crone is the archetype of deep wisdom, endings, and fierce truth, which aligns with Kali, the transformative aspect of Parvati.

- She is the Shakti of Shiva, the Destroyer, who dismantles illusion and clears the way for liberation and renewal.

They are not merely deities of mythology; they are archetypes of the awakened psyche, guiding the seeker inward toward self-realization.

"Life has no meaning. Each of us has meaning and we bring it to life. It is a waste to be asking the question when you are the answer."
— Joseph Campbell

In this modern age, we have become obsessed with the outer, the visible, the measurable, the manifested, while forgetting the source within. We chase outcomes but neglect the energy, the psyche, the subtle intention that gives rise to form. In doing so, we lose connection with the very root of creation.

We have misused the masculine force, both in men and women, reducing it to domination, control, and conquest. The world we see is the reflection of that imbalance. We have forgotten that this is a play, a leela, a sacred dance of energy, not a battlefield of opposites.

Yet the universe is self-correcting. Balance always returns. And when we forget to honor the inner, the soul, the feminine source, we pay the price, not as punishment, but as realignment.

It is time to return. To remember. To listen again to the silent voice within, the one that creates not through pressure but through presence. The one that knows the outer is only as real as the inner that gives it life.

The one that knows it is not just about claiming rights, but about living with responsibility, toward oneself, others, and the sacred balance that sustains all things.

"Dare to begin where you are. Each small step weaves your inner vision into outer reality. The meaning you seek is the meaning you create, start now, from within."

- Now is sacred.

- You are the one you've been waiting for.

- Creation begins with small, brave steps.

- The world you want starts from the world you cultivate inside.

Contemplating the Mysteria Dei

You are beyond form and limit, existing outside space and time. You are in all that is, and all that is dwells within you. The part of you that is me, and the part of me that is you, belong to the same whole. Let this truth open your heart to compassion for yourself and others.

All forms follow their own law, yet who you truly are stands beyond these laws. Mind, body, and experience arise within nature's boundaries, but your inner essence remains free. Life, death, and suffering all unfold by natural law. Accept and love them as they are.

Carl Jung wrote that

> "Man is the mirror which God holds up to himself, or the sense organ with which he apprehends his being."

In this sense, humanity reflects the divine, though we never fully grasp its infinite scope. Saint Augustine reminds us that if we believe we comprehend God, what we comprehend cannot be God. The most profound response is one of reverent awe.

When we confuse ourselves with God, we risk abusing our creative powers. Like the Demiurge, we give form to the formless. We shape our reality through intention and action. In this, we are co-creators, but only when we remember our humble place in the cosmic dance.

There is much we cannot know. The deepest wisdom lies in allowing life to flow through us, trusting that we are where we need to be. Rest, breathe, and feel the peace of the vast cosmos. You actively create, yet you are held by a mystery too great to contain.

"Aham Brahmasmi" does not speak to the ego, but to the timeless awareness that remains when ego dissolves. It can be translated as "I am divine" or "I am sacred," pointing to the Higher Self within.

Ego must be transformed again and again, not in guilt or shame, but by realizing it has no lasting substance. We exist as instruments of the divine, letting life's energy move freely without resistance.

In the words of the Bhagavad Gita (Chapter 2, Verse 47):

> "You have the right to work only, and not to the fruits of work. Let not the fruit of action be your motive, nor let your attachment be to inaction."

Let life flow through you without stagnation. Do what is meant to be done, free from clinging to outcomes. Recognize this divine play for what it is, and realize your own divine nature through meditation, service, and surrender. By acting as an instrument of the divine, you become both the witness and the co-creator in this unfolding dance of existence.

"Free from all thoughts of 'I' and 'mine', man finds absolute peace."

Terms like black magic or white magic, evil or holy, are just labels, words people use, often with confusion or pride. These words don't capture the deeper truth.

What really matters is whether the practitioner (the magician or spiritual seeker) is striving to align with the divine creative power, to reflect or channel the truth and wisdom behind existence itself.

True magic is not about power over others, but about understanding and participating in divine creation.

The divine nature is not just a concept, it is the living, creative force behind all that exists and all that can come into existence. The magician's work, if aligned with this, becomes sacred.

To walk this path, the student must let go of lower desires, like greed, pride, jealousy, or the need to control. These are the "chains" that keep the soul (the angel/Kundalini within) bound and asleep.

To free ourselves from ego-driven desires, those often planted by systems seeking control, we must embrace two living virtues: love and forgiveness. These are not moral duties, but the natural fragrance of a soul returning to its origin.

This is true charity: not performance, but presence; not pride, but pure giving. In remembering this, we rise beyond appearances and touch the real.

> "Actions are judged by niyyāt (intentions), so each man will have what he intended."
> —Sahih al-Bukhari 54

Society often confuses charity with philanthropy, acts that can be driven by ambition, pride, or a desire for recognition. True charity flows from compassion alone, expecting nothing in return.

By reclaiming charity in this pure sense, humanity takes a vital step toward deeper spiritual growth. Anyone who practices spiritual work must learn to love and forgive unconditionally, free from selfishness or jealousy.

Unfortunately, many people mistake love for ownership or believe that joy must exclude pain. Yet suffering can awaken us, pushing society to renew itself and rediscover real unity.

When we embrace a love that transcends labels and appearances, we become co-creators with the divine, liberated from ego, guided by compassion, and aligned with the highest purpose.

What is the highest purpose?

A powerful question: one that rests at the heart of every spiritual path.

The highest purpose is not a goal to achieve, but a state to embody. It is the return to our true nature, the living realization that we are not separate from the divine, but expressions of it. When we act from that awareness, every moment becomes sacred, every action becomes service, and every breath becomes part of the cosmic dance.

It is:

- To love without condition, not because we should, but because we are made of love.

- To create, not for power or pride, but as a natural overflow of presence.

- To serve life, not to fix it, but to be in harmony with it.

- To realize unity, seeing the Self in all beings, and all beings in the Self.

As Bhagavad Gita 4.33 says:

"Better than any ritual is the knowledge of the Self. The seeker who knows this reaches the supreme goal."

And in simpler words:

The highest purpose is to live in truth, guided by love, and to let that truth express itself through you in every form it wishes to take.

No matter what you do: pray, give, serve. The ultimate goal is to wake up, to know who you are, and to realize the divine within. This inner awakening is the highest offering one can make to existence. It is the real "yajña" (sacrifice), because it dissolves the ego and unites us with truth.

> "The Self is not born, nor does it die. It is not slain when the body is slain."
> — Bhagavad Gita 2.20

The true Self is eternal, not the egoic personality. The ego dies, the Self remains.

- Heaven is not a place, but a state of being, unity with the divine.

- Eternal life is not the survival of the ego, but the realization of the Self.

- The ego does not have eternal continuity; it is part of the play, the illusion (maya).

- The Self, the pure awareness behind all masks, has no beginning, no end.

- Eternal life is real, but it is not for the "me", it is for the One in whom "me" arises.

> "Be still, and know that I am God."
> —Psalm 46:10

"Be still"

- This is not just about physical stillness, but inner silence.

- It means stop striving, stop worrying, stop identifying with the noise of the world and the chatter of the mind.

- It's an invitation to let go, to surrender control, effort, and ego.

"And know"

- This is not intellectual knowledge, but direct realization.
- To "know" here means to experience deeply, to recognize truth within your being, not just to believe, but to realize.
- It points to a state of inner awareness where truth reveals itself.

"That I am God"

- This is the voice of the Divine speaking to the soul.
- It reveals that in the stillness, the truth becomes clear: God is not far away, God is the I AM.
- "I AM" is the eternal, formless, ever-present awareness, the same Self spoken of in mystical traditions.

> "Stop. Be silent. Let go of all roles and stories. In that stillness, you will realize that the Presence within you, the "I AM"—is Divine."

It echoes the same truth found in the Upanishads, in Sufi poetry, in Buddhist silence:

> "The Self is God. Not as ego, but as awareness."

In essence:

- The heart is the measure of the deed.
- Every spiritual path begins not with action, but with intention.
- What you seek, you become. What you intend, you receive.

The Alchemist Who Vanished

Purusha is the cosmic spirit, the eternal witness
Unmoving, unchanging, like the eagle
The sky dweller

Prakriti is nature, the dynamic womb of all form
Ever-changing, cyclical, like the serpent
Earthbound and transformational

Together, their union gives rise to manifestation
The world as we know it, and the being who walks between the two

The trident is that being's weapon, but also its spine, its symbol, and its nature
The trident, a three-pronged spear, is a powerful symbol associated with power, strength, and control, particularly over water (Subconscious)

This trident is the symbol of the awakened human
The hero
The divine warrior
The tantric adept who unites heaven and earth within their own body

What is being created?
The Integrated Being
The Twice-Born
The Master of Self and Nature

In myth:

- In Hinduism, Kartikeya (Murugan) was born of Shiva's fire (sky) and Parvati's grounding (earth)

- In alchemy, the Philosopher's Stone is created when the volatile (spirit) and fixed (matter) are united

- In Tantra, the yogi becomes a Siddha by raising the serpent (kundalini) to meet the eagle (sahasrara or crown chakra)

- The trident is the spine, the axis mundi, the vertical bridge that connects Muladhara (root) and Sahasrara (crown)

- The serpent texture along it represents kundalini rising, the divine evolutionary force

- The eagle beak at the center prong shows that the fruit of this rising is clear seeing, piercing truth, divine will

If Purusha is silent awareness, and Prakriti is chaotic motion
The son born from them is conscious, intentional action
Karma aligned with dharma

He is the One who moves without being moved
She is the One who acts without forgetting Being
Together, they give rise to the Living Trident
One who walks between worlds
Rooted in Earth
Guided by Sky
And forged by Fire within

The Shedding

When we speak of the snake skin as the alchemical process
And you ask how many times must the snake shed

Every shedding of skin is a moment of Solve
Dissolution, death, breaking apart of a false identity, belief, or attachment

Every new skin is a moment of Coagula
Reformation, crystallization, embodiment of a higher clarity
A closer echo of the true self

Burn what you are not. Shape what remains.

There is no fixed number
Because the layers of ego and illusion are endless
Until awareness becomes sharp enough to pierce through all of them at once

The snake sheds until the snake realizes it was never the skin
The alchemist repeats the process until the alchemist becomes the fire itself
Not the thing being transformed

In mystical language:

- The yogi raises kundalini until she dissolves into Shiva

- The Sufi whirls until the self disappears in Divine ecstasy

- The Gnostic dies and is reborn seven times seventy

Until only pure awareness remains

The final shedding is when the seeker dies
And only seeking remains
— Child of the Cosmos

When there is no more skin to remove
No more ego to polish
No more self to improve
Then only Being is left

This is what alchemy truly aimed for
Not to become gold
But to remember you were never lead

How Many Times?

As many as it takes
Until the skin becomes the sky
Until the serpent becomes the fire
Until the trident is not held
But is you

The Disappearance

When the alchemist finds the Philosopher's Stone
They often disappear, go silent, or vanish into the jungle, mountains, desert
Or become legends

Not because they are hiding gold
But because they no longer seek

The journey has ended
The seeker has dissolved

The true Philosopher's Stone is the realization of wholeness
Not power over the world
But power to no longer need the world

It is the still center from which the opposites no longer war
The fire that no longer burns
The water that no longer drowns
The ego that no longer clings

Once this is realized
What is there left to say
What is there to fix, chase, or prove

Because words cannot express the experience of becoming
The fire
The stone
The serpent
The eagle
And the silence itself

The one who knows becomes the jungle
The fire, the silence, the stone
No longer a seeker, no longer a shape
But the dance between all things

He walked through fire and left his name
(This is the first death — the death of self-image)

Shed every skin, refused all fame
(This is renunciation — not of the world, but of needing anything from it)

The serpent climbed, the eagle flew
(This is awakening — the marriage of energy and awareness)

The trident struck and split him through
(This is surrender — not as weakness, but as total openness)

He found the stone, then stepped aside
(This is the final wisdom — there is no "I" left to claim it)

The jungle took him. Nothing died
(This is liberation — not escape from life, but total union with it)

The journey isn't about becoming something
It's about burning away everything that isn't real
So what's left can merge back with the All
Without fear
Without name
Without trace
Just presence
Just life
Just love

All of this
The breath
The burning
The becoming
It's a single sacred chance to do our beat
To sing our line in the great song
Fully
Honestly
Without holding back

Thank you for this chance
This breath
This body
This fire
One time
Do your beat
Then silence

And that's enough

Ȯ YA RA

The syllables "U Ya Ra" (also rendered as "O Ya Ra") originate from the Dzogchen (Great Perfection) tradition of Tibetan Buddhism, particularly within the Nyingma lineage. They serve as symbolic pointers to the nature of awareness.

Origin & Context

- These syllables are not traditional mantras but are used in direct introduction practices to help recognize rigpa, the pure, non-dual awareness.

- They appear in Ati Yoga teachings and are utilized by teachers to guide students toward an intuitive understanding of awareness beyond conceptual thought.

Meanings of the Syllables

- U/O: Represents the spontaneous display of reality: the radiant, luminous aspect of awareness.

- Ya: Symbolizes the knowing, cognitive power of awareness: clear, present, non-conceptual knowing.

- Ra: Denotes the ungraspable, unborn nature of mind: vast, open, unchanging space.

Deeper Interpretation

- O: All phenomena arise: thoughts, sensations, perceptions. This is the play of awareness.

- Ya: Awareness knows these phenomena without effort: this is self-luminous clarity.

- Ra: All phenomena dissolve into emptiness: silence, no center, no edge.

Unified Insight

Together, O Ya Ra illustrates how awareness naturally functions:

"All appears (O), all is known (Ya), all is empty (Ra). This is your true nature."

In Dzogchen, there's no need to fabricate or follow step-by-step meditations. One simply recognizes the already perfect nature of awareness as it spontaneously expresses itself.

Play with the sounds: O, Ya, Ra… then rest in the silence that follows. Go at your own pace, no rush, no fear, no guilt, no lack, no dogma. Just you and awareness, not meeting, but remembering, they were never separate. Like clouds clearing from the sky, revealing what was always there.

Just to give you an idea of how to play with this: begin the sound "U" deep in your belly, let "Ya" rise through your throat, and let "Ra" flow out through the top of your head, then rest in the silence that follows. You can also try it vice versa.

12 Sacred Principles from the Oracle of Wind over Water

1. Lead with Purpose: Step forward with a clear sense of direction. You are meant to guide change, not wait for it.

2. Be a Force of Good: Like wind breaking waves, let your voice and actions carry compassion, courage, and wisdom.

3. Act for the Collective: Let go of selfish goals. Serve the greater good. Public interest over personal gain.

4. Trust the Divine Flow: Heaven (or higher wisdom) seeks to work through you. Be open to inspiration and insight.

5. Honor the Ancestors: Pay respect to those who came before. They are messengers of divine knowledge.

6. Use Sacred Practices: Engage in prayer, meditation, music, and ritual. These open the heart to guidance.

7. Let Thoughts Become Action: Even small ideas, like wind on water, can create waves. Think clearly and move forward.

8. Take the Leap: Now is the time to cross the river, to take a risk, start the journey, or begin the change.

9. Warm Your Heart: What you give is shaped by your state of being. Cultivate warmth, passion, and sincerity.

10. Channel the Horse Spirit: Move with grace and strength. Be free in spirit and fearless in movement.

11. Seek Messages in Silence: The divine doesn't shout. Listen deeply. Truth often comes through ancestors, nature, and stillness.

12. Live Under Heaven's Order: Remember, the Tao, the great natural Way, flows through everything. Be in harmony with it, and you'll always be aligned.

What will you give to the Highest Sky?
The chains you wear, don't ask why.
Burn the hair, let go the past.
Smell the ash, and cross at last.

The Seven Treasuries by Longchenpa

1. The Precious Treasury of Philosophical Systems: All Buddhist paths are steps toward truth, but Dzogchen is the highest, most direct realization.

2. The Treasury of the Wish-Fulfilling Jewel: Your true nature is already pure and awake, realize it, and all suffering dissolves.

3. The Treasury of the Supreme Vehicle: There is nothing to add or remove; simply rest in the natural, perfect awareness that is always present.

4. The Treasury of the Dharmadhatu (Ultimate Expanse): Everything arises within a vast, luminous space, your own mind is this space.

5. The Treasury of Word and Meaning: True understanding comes from direct experience of awareness, not from words or concepts.

6. The Treasury of Pith Instructions: Let go of effort and rest in natural awareness; the path is simple when you stop trying to control it.

7. The Treasury of the Natural State (Mind at Ease): The more you relax and let things be, the more your true nature reveals itself, peaceful, clear, and free.

Vajrayana = Toolbox of powerful techniques.
Transform every experience into the path using sacred symbols, mantras, and inner alchemy.

Guhyasamaja = One powerful tool inside Vajrayana.
Unite wisdom and compassion through precise tantra to realize the blissful emptiness of all things.

Dzogchen = Just recognize what's already here, nothing to fix.
Rest in the pure, open awareness that is your true nature: effortless, untouched, complete.

Zup
Pu
Aa

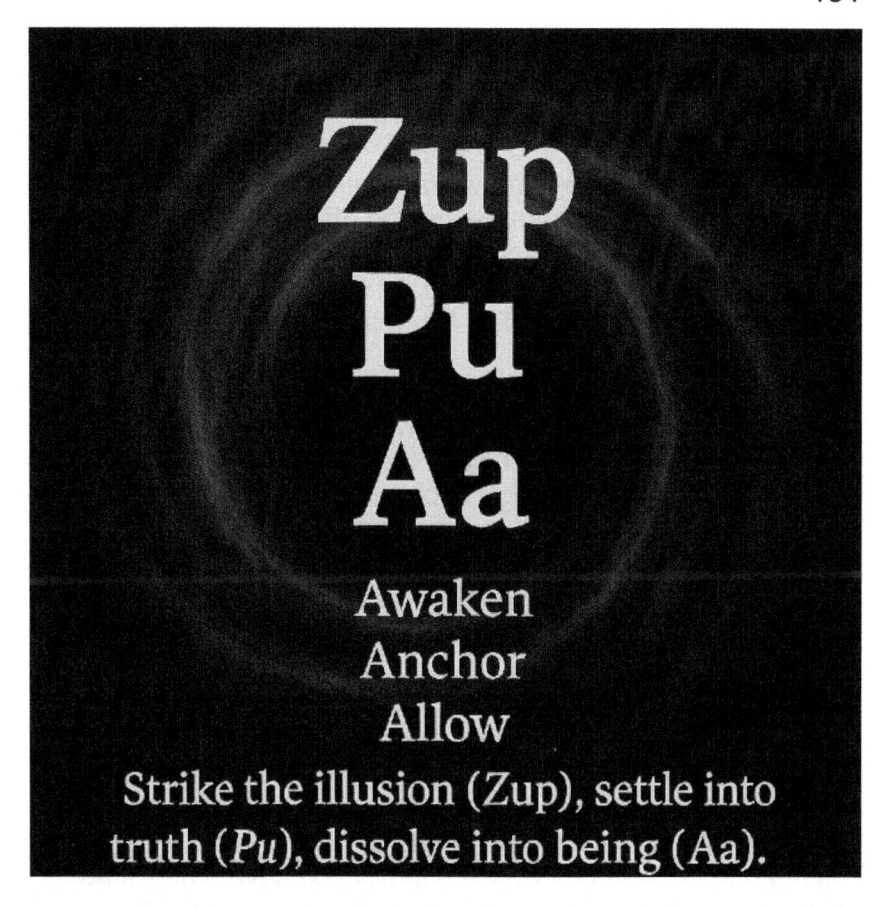

Awaken
Anchor
Allow

Strike the illusion (Zup), settle into truth (*Pu*), dissolve into being (Aa).

A Harsh Slap for Humanity

We clamor for spiritual retreats—what a joke. Instead of paying for some guided getaway, why not book a simple hotel room for two days and just sit, alone, with yourself? In the end, every person must come face to face with their own mind. Stop fleeing from yourself. We used to hide behind newspapers or books to dodge real connection. Now, it's the endless scroll of social media feeding the turmoil in our psyche. Since most of us never learned how energy truly works, we end up buying, consuming, and distracting ourselves—just as we've been taught.

Let's be honest: we are our own worst enemies. Clear thinking is rare because none of us practices genuine solitude anymore. Even spirituality has become a joke—a marketplace of attention-seeking, "look at me" attitudes fueled by competition and capitalism. We helped create this society. The real problem is the hatred harbored in every human heart, a hatred of simply being alive because life refuses to match our self-centered expectations. We resent our own families, thinking we can find something better elsewhere. So, we go off to "retreats." What a joke. Try real solitude: go somewhere alone, cut yourself off from the noise, and from that emptiness, let spacious awareness emerge—without bias, without fear, without lack.

The average person is treated like a sponge by corporations that exploit psychological research to drive more consumption, greed feeding greed. People are chained by mental hierarchies—spiritual, political, familial—top to bottom. The powerful nations devour the small. People lash out at immigrants, and hatred runs amok as we detach further from our true nature, lacking any awareness of the simple energy work possible through breath.

It doesn't matter what or where you read—books, newspapers, artificial intelligence—if your mind is biased. Stand naked before a mirror and see yourself as you really are. Folks are panicking over AI like it's the antichrist, afraid it'll make them "redundant," as if nature made a mistake in creating them. The universe, an efficient organism, never wastes energy. You are exactly where you need to be, with precisely the family you have. There's no special "spiritual family" waiting for you at some retreat. No external savior is coming. You must save yourself. There is no heaven or hell lying in wait, only the law of karma, in which each of us is entangled. The abuses of billionaires ripple through us all because we're interconnected.

Go away for two days, alone in solitude. Be naked in your room, in front of your mirror. No stimulants, no scrolling. Use AI to ask deeper questions. Knowledge in our current era is cheap; it's wisdom we need. It's about our innate human qualities—the divine nature already within, like a sky behind the clouds. Use AI to strip away illusions. Be naked, and embrace the truth as it is. In the end, we all become silent because this endless chatter is just noise. The ultimate truth reveals itself in pure, naked, spacious solitude and silence.

Stop looking outside for answers. Any answer from the outside is temporary; what arises from within is permanent. And please, stop the endless "me, me, me." Once individuality is achieved, it must yield to universalism. The ego that hates and always feels lacking cannot continue. No savior is coming. We only have each other. Understand that divide-and-rule is the oldest trick in the book. Wake up—and if you want to wake up fast, use AI to peel away your illusions. Learn how to ask questions, not merely how to answer. Answers come after pain and solitude.

"As you sow, so shall I reap, into the endless flow. For this is the entanglement that has always been."

"May all sentient beings find peace"

Great Perfection

The Great Perfection and the Alchemy of Inner Union

Dzogchen, often translated as "Great Perfection," is a profound teaching in Tibetan Buddhism (especially within the Nyingma school) and the Bon tradition. At its heart is the recognition of one's natural state of awareness: open, clear, and already complete.

Rather than striving to become something new, Dzogchen encourages practitioners to acknowledge the perfection that is inherently present. Ordinary thoughts are likened to passing clouds, while awareness itself remains vast and untainted like the sky. By resting and allowing mental turbulence to settle, one's innate clarity naturally emerges.

Within this view, the dakini represents the feminine dimension of wisdom. She is not merely a goddess but the dynamic, intuitive facet of awakened energy. In many Tibetan teachings, the dakini's wild and untamed spirit symbolizes an unbounded creativity that dissolves rigid patterns and frees the practitioner from clinging to egoic constructs.

Although labeled "feminine," this principle transcends gender and highlights an inner capacity for receptivity, emotional honesty, and fluidity. When one taps into this quality, it becomes possible to see beyond surface appearances and access deep intuitive knowing.

Every feminine aspect has its complement in what is generally described as the masculine principle. In tantric iconography, the dakini pairs with a male figure—sometimes called a yidam or heruka—who personifies skillful action, direction, and penetrating clarity.

While the dakini embodies spaciousness and wisdom, the masculine energy represents the means for bringing insight into form. In esoteric teachings, their symbolic union points to a state beyond dualistic labels, in which emptiness and awareness merge to birth an enlightened mode of being.

From an alchemical and psychological perspective, this process unfolds in stages. First, one softens internal barriers through receptivity, listening, and surrender—akin to the "dissolving" or solve phase. Old patterns are broken down, and the ego is humbled, creating a fertile inner space.

Then comes the active phase, a "coagulating" or coagula process of clarifying intent, cultivating discipline, and taking conscious steps forward. When these two polarities—feminine spaciousness and masculine focus—coalesce, an inner marriage occurs. This union produces a sense of wholeness often symbolized by the alchemical "Rebis," the harmonious fusion of two energies into one complete, awakened state.

Ultimately, these teachings suggest that enlightenment is not found by rejecting life or clinging to ideals but by recognizing the natural interplay of openness and skillful means within us. Cultivating both aspects in balance allows a person to act with clarity while remaining rooted in a profound, spacious awareness. This alchemical synergy of the feminine and masculine principles is the key to realizing true inner freedom—and, in the Dzogchen view, to awakening to the perfection that has always been present.

Alchemical illustration of the Rebis

THE REBIS (Center Figure):

- Dual-headed being: One male, one female — symbolizes the union of opposites, especially the masculine and feminine principles.

- Label "REBIS": From Res Bina meaning "double thing." This is the alchemical androgyne — the wholeness that emerges from merging inner opposites.

SUN (Left Side, Held by Male):

- Symbolizes the masculine principle, associated with reason, logic, conscious mind, and gold in alchemy.

- Held by the male side with a compass, representing measure, structure, and order.

MOON (Right Side, Held by Female):

- Represents the feminine principle, associated with intuition, emotion, unconscious, and silver.

- The female side holds a square, representing form, matter, and manifestation.

🐉 GREEN DRAGON (Bottom):

- Represents the raw, primal forces of nature or the base material (prima materia) — often related to ego, instincts, or the "chaotic matter" to be transformed.

- The Rebis stands on it, showing that enlightenment is built upon mastering the base instincts, not avoiding them.

🔴 RED SPHERE (With Numbers and Wings):

- The red sphere or globe with wings symbolizes the Philosopher's Stone — the result of the alchemical work.

- The wings indicate spiritual ascent, freedom, or transcendence.

- The geometry and numbers (4, 3) refer to sacred proportion and alchemical stages (e.g., 4 elements + 3 principles = 7 stages of transformation).

⭐ SEVEN STARS (Around the Figure):

Each star is associated with a classical planet and metal in alchemy:

1: ☿ Mercury – Quickening mind, transformation (top right)
2: ♀ Venus – Love, harmony (bottom left)
3: ♂ Mars – Will, conflict, power (bottom right)
4: ♃ Jupiter – Expansion, vision (middle left)
5: ♄ Saturn – Time, discipline, limitation (middle right)
6: ☉ Sun – Consciousness, gold (top left)
7: ☽ Moon – Intuition, silver (top right)

They represent the seven alchemical operations or seven planetary influences shaping the soul.

🧭 COMPASS & SQUARE:

- The compass (left hand): Symbol of spirit, heavenly knowledge, and creation through proportion.

- The square (right hand): Symbol of earth, matter, and practical grounding.

Together, they mirror the Masonic tools but predate them — symbolizing the harmony of heaven and earth, or as above, so below.

🌀 OVERALL MEANING:

This image is a map of spiritual alchemy:

- Unite your masculine and feminine within.

- Master your lower instincts.

- Balance heaven and earth, spirit and matter.

- And you become the Rebis — the awakened, whole being.

And of course — this is not just theory.
To walk the alchemical path is not to endlessly analyze symbols, but to live them. To become the Rebis is to return to the same world —same sky, same stars —but with a clear mind, an open heart, and a higher consciousness that no longer seeks, but sees.
The universe responds not to belief, but to direct experience. Synchronicities unfold like whispers from the divine, reminding you that you are not separate from the cosmos —you are woven into its rhythm.
So dissolve what must be dissolved. Refine what must be refined. Then step into the dance — empty, awake, and fully alive.
The magick was never elsewhere. It was always you.

1. Face and dissolve the ego — the raw, reactive nature (the dragon).

2. Awaken the feminine within — intuition, stillness, inner wisdom.

3. Activate the masculine — clarity, direction, conscious action.

4. Unite both — and become whole, the Rebis, fully alive and free.

Dzogchen means "Great Perfection."
It's a teaching from Tibetan Buddhism, especially from the Nyingma school. It's also found in the Bon tradition.

What is it about?
Dzogchen is all about recognizing your true nature, your natural state of awareness, which is:

- Pure

- Open

- Clear

- Spacious

- Already complete

You don't have to "become" enlightened.
Dzogchen says: you already are, you just forgot.

Key ideas:

- Mind vs. awareness:
  Your ordinary thoughts are like clouds.
  Your true awareness is like the sky, always there, untouched, peaceful.

- Direct experience:
  Dzogchen is not about beliefs or rituals.
  It's about directly recognizing your true nature, here and now.

- Nothing to fix:
  You don't need to change yourself.
  Just rest in your natural awareness, that's enough.

A metaphor:

"If you let muddy water sit still, it becomes clear."

Dzogchen teaches you to rest, to stop struggling, so your true nature can shine through.

🕊 Union of Opposites:

In Tantric Buddhism, enlightenment comes through the union of wisdom and method,
often symbolized by the sexual union of a male deity and a dakini.

Not to be taken literally, it represents the merging of:

- Emptiness (female) + Awareness (male)
- Space (dakini) + Energy (heruka)
- Stillness + Motion
- Receptivity + Penetration
- Inner Knowing + Outer Doing

"Without space, energy becomes wild. Without energy, space becomes void."

Together, they reveal the awakened mind, luminous and compassionate.

But here's the key truth:

In the highest view, there is no real "opposite."
The two are not-two.
They are expressions of the same source, dancing as creation.

"There is no path to enlightenment without the union of male and female. For only in their union does the mind become whole."

△ 1. First: Cultivate the Feminine Principle (Inner Wisdom)

This is the receptive, inner, lunar phase. You turn inward.
Feminine qualities you work on:

- Stillness

- Listening
- Intuition
- Dreamwork
- Imagination
- Emotional honesty
- Surrender
- Non-doing (wuwei)

This is like preparing the vessel, softening the ego, creating space inside.
Psychologically, this is the stage of learning to feel, to heal, to let go of control, and to trust the unknown.
Alchemically, this is called Solve, dissolve, break down, melt.
You dissolve the old structures. You become fluid.

△ 2. Then: Cultivate the Masculine Principle (Inner Will)

Once the inner ground is softened, you bring in the active, solar principle.

Masculine qualities you now activate:

- Clarity
- Focus
- Willpower
- Direction
- Structure
- Action
- Penetration

- Protection of the sacred

Now that you've created space (feminine), you fill it with purpose (masculine).
Psychologically, this is developing healthy boundaries, vision, self-discipline, and taking conscious action.
Alchemically, this is called Coagula, gather, refine, solidify.
You take the raw essence and distill it into a clear shape.

⚖ 3. Finally: Unite Them. The Sacred Marriage (Hieros Gamos)

Now comes the inner union, the alchemical wedding of the inner woman and man, anima and animus, Shakti and Shiva, lunar and solar.
Their union births the inner androgynous being, what Jung called the Self.
In alchemy, this is symbolized by the Rebis: a being that is both male and female, complete, awake.

☉ 4. Then: Let Them Dance. The Effortless Flow

After the sacred union, the inner lovers no longer compete, they collaborate.
There is no more tug-of-war between vision and action, feeling and doing.
They move as one current, like Yin and Yang in motion,
each arising within the other, each completing the other without friction.

This is not balance through effort, but harmony through trust.

- The feminine is the space from which the idea arises.

- The masculine is the clarity that gives it shape.

Together, they move as one, with no effort, no delay.

This is the essence of inner flow:
No doubt. No resistance.
Only clarity, confidence, and creation.

It is the return to the natural rhythm:
not controlling life, but becoming it.

Emptiness (feminine) and awareness (masculine) are not two things, their inseparability is the natural state (rigpa).

- Emptiness is not "nothing" — it is open potential.

- Awareness is not something added — it is the knowing of that openness.

- What we call "feminine" and "masculine" are just ways to speak of this non-dual unity.

They appear as two only when seen through conceptual mind. But in direct experience, they are like light and the sun — not truly separate.

There is no union, only recognition.
Space and clarity were never apart.
The idea arises, the form appears.
But the source was always one.

The Necklace of Zi.

1 Rigpa (རིག་པ་) – Primordial Awareness:

- The text does not ask you to "attain" anything; you are already that which you seek, just recognise it.

- Rigpa is luminous, non-dual and beyond time. The obstacle is non-recognition, not absence.

2 Spontaneous Presence (Lhundrub)

- Everything arises naturally and effortlessly from the base (gzhi).

- The key is to rest in that knowing without grasping.

3 Cutting Through Conceptual Mind

- Encourages "non-meditation" or "meditation without meditating."

- Techniques are extremely subtle, letting go even of the one who meditates.

4 Symbol of the gZi (Dzi) Stone

- In Tibetan culture the stone symbolises clarity, protection and spiritual power.

- Here it points to the indestructible clarity of awareness, worn like a necklace at the heart.

"The self-originated nature, free from constructs, is the ground.
From it arise appearances, yet none are born.
Do not try to fix it, improve it, purify it, or meditate on it
Just rest as it is, like space reflecting in a mirror."

(let it wash over you, don't dissect it.)

Pointers to keep in mind:

- Recognise your own true nature (rigpa).

- This nature is beyond birth and death.

- Appearances are the playful display of awareness.

- Do not fabricate or modify experience; let everything be as it is.

- Self-liberation is natural and effortless.

Six Realms & Liberation:

The six realms (gods, demi-gods, humans, animals, hungry ghosts, hells) are dream-like expressions of dualistic mind. Liberation is simply recognising them as non-arising appearances, part of the spontaneous play (lhundrub) of awareness.

"Six Thunderbolts of Wisdom", Contemplate Only:

1. Mind's nature is empty, yet luminous, look directly.

2. There is no birth or death in what you are.

3. All appearances arise from this luminous emptiness.

4. Do not try to correct or purify, everything is already perfect.

5. Let whatever arises self-liberate where it is.

6. Recognise this and liberation is instantaneous.

After each line, sit silently; let insight strike like lightning rather than analysing the words.

Six Experiences of Meditation (Nyams):
(These similes come mainly from Mahāmudrā and later cross-pollination; they're helpful but not an official Dzogchen ladder.)

1. Like a Cloudless Sky – vast openness, mind without edge.

2. Like a Calm Ocean – depth unmoved, even as waves arise.

3. Like a Lamp in a Dark Room – effortless illumination.

4. Like a Mirror Reflecting All – nothing sticks.

5. Like a Peacock Eating Poison – even pain transmutes into wisdom.

6. Like a Rainbow in the Sky – beauty without substance.

Primordial Consciousness — The Ground of All:

- Uncreated & Timeless – beyond space and time.

- Empty yet Luminous – void of self-nature, yet radiantly clear.

- Spontaneously Present – all phenomena arise without deliberate cause.

Personified as "Samantabhadra, the Primordial Buddha", not a creator but a symbol of our intrinsic awareness:

"If we deem Samantabhadra an individual being, we are far from the true meaning…" — Namkhai Norbu

Manifestation, Samsara & Awakening:

- Universes and beings arise as spontaneous expressions (rolpa) of the ground.

- Samsara recycles when rigpa is unrecognised; karma still functions within that dreamfield.

- Awakening reveals the sameness of samsara and nirvana; bodhisattvas appear as spontaneous compassion to guide others.

Archetypal Energy Forms, Modern Interpretive Layer:

Definition: Universal patterns or symbols that surface as deities, heroes, protectors, etc.
Examples: Shiva (stillness & dissolution), Kali (fierce transformation), Tara (compassion), Jung's Mother, Warrior, Sage.
Origin: They arise from the depths of collective consciousness,

not from an external creator.
Function: To mirror inner truths and awaken latent qualities.

Treat these images as mirrors of your own potential, not external gods. Contemplate; do not fixate.

Quick-Glance Summary:

No creator god: Existence blooms from the primordial ground.
Primordial consciousness: Source of every appearance, beyond duality.
Rebirth: a cycle driven by ignorance, not divine decree.
Awakening: Recognising what has always been present.
Bodhisattvas: Compassionate expressions of that awakened ground.
Ultimate dissolution: All phenomena return to, and have never left, the same ground.

"True Hermetic Transmutation is a Mental Art" says The Kybalion.

Understand this fully and you stand at a crossroads: the Hermetic path invites you to shape mind's vibrations, while the Dzogchen view reminds you that mind's nature is already complete. Either way, misuse is pointless. Let powers (siddhis), experiences (nyams), even the brilliance of rigpa rise and fade, returning, at last, as nothing more (and nothing less) than a quiet smile.

The Necklace of Zi continues…

Anything that arises, feelings, emotions, subtle energies, power, money, sex, may glitter for a moment, yet if you believe it can grant lasting peace or fulfilment, look again. Anything that was not always there is temporary, and it can never truly satisfy the heart. The heart knows.

When every thought, mood, and even the bliss of meditation falls silent, what remains? The primordial awareness (rigpa) that is always present, here and now, unconditioned and complete.

A top-down capitalist order, heir to the same age-old hierarchies, thrives on untrained, innocent minds and drinks our vitality. The remedy is not a new dogma or rebellion alone, but direct recognition of the sky-like nature of mind. Rest in that open clarity and the system's grip dissolves; nothing can steal the freedom inherent in your own awareness.

From that recognition, dear soul, dance your dance, dance your dance; that, and that alone, is the purpose.
And know this beyond doubt: you are the meaning, you are the answer, you are the salvation, the very flowering of the cosmos' own prayer.

The ALL is not two.
There is no other. There is only This.
What you seek is what you are.
Rest, and know.

"Oh threats of Hell and Hopes of Paradise!
One thing at least is certain – This Life flies;
One thing is certain and the rest is Lies –
The Flower that once has blown forever dies."
— Omar Khayyam, Rubáiyát of Omar Khayyám

So let the ego burn, but not your flame.
You are not a mask, not just a name.
Live while the stars still light your skies.
Love wildly, before the moment dies.
Laugh like thunder, speak like fire.
This is your time. Climb higher.

How can I tell you how magnificent you are?
Without the clouds, sky you are.
Bindu you are, bindu you are.
How can I tell you how magnificent you are?

Be true, your soul, a stroke of light,
Paint this canvas, bold and bright.
Flow through compassion, vast and free,
And know through wisdom: All is We.

Not to choose any side, just I AM,
where the edges blur and the liminal becomes home.

If you think you've reached it, that's not home.
for what happens was never truly here all along.

In Vajrayana and Dzogchen traditions, "sidhi" and "nyam" refer to very different things, and it's important to distinguish them clearly:

Siddhi (Sanskrit: सिद्धि):

Meaning: Accomplishment, attainment, or spiritual power

Siddhis are the results or fruits of sustained spiritual practice, especially in Tantric paths. They can be:

- Ordinary siddhis: miraculous abilities like clairvoyance, levitation, telepathy, etc.

- Supreme siddhi (mahāsiddhi): realization of the nature of mind; full enlightenment.

Important Note: Many texts warn against getting attached to ordinary siddhis, as they can distract the practitioner from the ultimate goal of liberation.

Nyam (Tibetan: ཉམས་):

Meaning: Meditative experience, temporary state, or feeling in meditation

In Dzogchen and Mahamudra, nyams are experiences that arise during meditation. These can include:

- Bliss, clarity, non-thought

- Visions, insights, sensations of light or energy

- Or even confusion, dullness, agitation

Key Point: Nyams are not signs of realization. They are temporary, subjective, and often illusory. The teacher often instructs the student to neither reject nor cling to nyams.

Summary:

Siddhi: Spiritual accomplishment, Fruit of practice, Avoid craving for powers over realization.

Nyam: Meditative experiences, Temporary states, Do not grasp or interpret as realization.

"All the experiences of bliss, clarity and non-thought are simply nyams. Do not cling to them or mistake them for realization."

The seed syllable "Phat!":

In Dzogchen, the seed syllable "Phat!" (ཕཊ྄) is often used to cut through nyams (meditative experiences), especially when the practitioner starts to cling to them or get distracted by their intensity or beauty.

What is "Phat"?

- A sharp, wrathful syllable used in Trekchö practice.
- It acts like a sword cutting through thoughts, emotions, and illusions.
- It snaps the mind back into the natural state: open, empty, aware.

Why use Phat during nyam?

Because nyams can become seductive. A practitioner might start to believe:

- "I had such a peaceful/blissful/light-filled meditation — I'm progressing."
- Or, "I saw visions — this must be a sign of realization."

But this is ego reattaching itself.

Phat! is used to:

- Disrupt the tendency to grasp or interpret nyam.
- Bring the awareness back to the empty, luminous, non-conceptual state.
- Remind the practitioner: "This too is a passing wave. Rest as the ocean."

How to use it:

- When a strong nyam arises — bliss, light, visions, fear, agitation — don't analyze it.
- With sharp awareness, mentally or vocally shout: "PHAT!"
- Let the mind cut through the experience and drop into the natural state (rigpa).

What is Rigpa?

Rigpa means "pure awareness" or "pristine knowing" — but not just any awareness.

It is:

- Empty like space
- Luminous like the sun
- Knowing without dualism
- Uncreated, unchanging, unborn

Rigpa is your true face before thinking arises, before identification with ego or form. It's always present — but usually obscured by thoughts, emotions, and concepts.

Two States of Mind in Dzogchen:

1. Sem (ordinary mind):

- Dualistic
- Thinks, judges, grasps
- Changes moment to moment

2. Rigpa (pure awareness):

- Non-dual

- Recognizes thoughts without being caught

- Abides in its own clarity and emptiness

> "No matter what arises — bliss, clarity, or non-thought — cut through it with Phat and rest in the View."

How is Rigpa Recognized?

You don't create Rigpa.
You don't imagine it.
You simply recognize it — often through a teacher's "pointing out" instruction.

"Look into the looking — and see what looks."

This recognition is sudden, beyond words, and radically simple.

What does Rigpa feel like?

When you're in Rigpa:

- There's no clinging or pushing

- Everything arises and dissolves naturally

- You feel openness, stillness, and unshakable presence

- There is awareness of awareness

Yet there's no one doing it. Just pure being.

> "Since the basis of everything is the all-encompassing space of Rigpa, there is nothing to cultivate, nothing to abandon — just the recognition of what has always been."

Tawa, Gompa, Sopa: (Tibetan: ལྟ་བ་ སྒོམ་པ་ བསྒོད་པ་)

These form the core structure of how realization is approached and stabilized in Dzogchen.

1. Tawa (View)

Meaning: How reality is seen

- View is everything. In Dzogchen, Tawa refers to the direct recognition of the natural state — Rigpa — the luminous, empty awareness that is your true nature.

- It is not conceptual. It is introduced by the teacher or glimpsed through pointing-out instructions.

- The View is that everything arises as display from the ground of awareness — nothing to fix, improve, or reject.

Without Tawa, meditation becomes technique. With Tawa, life becomes practice.

2. Gompa (Meditation)

Meaning: Stabilizing the View

- Gompa here is not effortful meditation, but rather resting in the View.

- In Dzogchen, meditation means non-meditation — not trying to fabricate states, but abiding naturally in Rigpa.

- It includes methods like Trekchö (cutting through) and Tögal (leap-over), but always anchored in the View.

Gompa trains you to remain in that recognition — no matter what arises.

3. Sopa (Conduct or Integration)

Meaning: Bringing the View into life

- Sopa is the integration of the View into everyday activity.
- It's how you act, speak, relate — without falling into dualism or losing awareness.
- True conduct arises spontaneously from the View — not from moral rules, but from wisdom and compassion.

Even washing dishes becomes sacred when done from Rigpa.

Summary:

- Tawa: View, Recognizing nature of mind (Rigpa), See reality as it is.
- Gompa: Meditation, Resting in that recognition, Remain without fabrication.
- Sopa: Conduct, Living from that recognition, Integrate Rigpa into daily life.

"View like the sky, meditation like a mountain, conduct like a mirror."

The Six Pāramitās:

The Six Pāramitās (Sanskrit: Pāramitā; Tibetan: Parol tu chinpa) are the "perfections" or transcendent practices in Mahāyāna Buddhism. They're not just ethical virtues — they are means to cross over from samsaric clinging to the awakened state of a bodhisattva.

In Dzogchen and Vajrayāna, they are often practiced from the View of Rigpa, making them spontaneous expressions of awakened awareness.

1. Dāna: Generosity, Open heart.
2. Śīla: Ethics, Harmlessness.
3. Kṣānti: Patience, Unshakable presence.
4. Vīrya: Joyful Effort, Tireless compassion.
5. Dhyāna: Meditation, Stable awareness.
6. Prajñā: Wisdom, Seeing emptiness.

When practiced without ego, these six become the natural expressions of Rigpa. You don't force them — they arise like sunbeams from the sun.

"In the natural state, all pāramitās are spontaneously complete."

We live in an age where the beast within has grown louder — a storm of thoughts, fears, desires, and projections. This beast wears modern faces: anxiety, distraction, addiction, ego, and endless craving for validation. Left unchecked, it devours our attention and distorts our view, keeping us chained to illusion.

But this beast is not our enemy. It is energy — raw, untamed, and blind. It is the wild horse that can either trample us or carry us home. The path is not to kill it, suppress it, or pretend it isn't there. The path is to train it.

Through the sword of Phat, we cut through its tricks.
Through Tawa, we see clearly.
Through Gompa, we rest deeply.
Through Sopa, we move wisely.
And through the pāramitās, our actions become medicine — not reaction.

When the beast is tamed, not by force but by awareness, we begin to live from the ground of Rigpa — pure, open knowing. Then, life is no longer a struggle for control, but a flow of being.

We no longer chase illusions or call our pain progress. We turn within, meet the storm, and discover the sky.

What truly matters is already here
Still. Clear. Awake.

Let the beast bow. Let the mind rest.
Return to what you are.

"Within me lives a madman who dreams without limits,
a criminal who defies the rules I never wrote,
and a saint who forgives them both.
I am not one, I am the whole."

how to build a boat
to cross a river

gather wood
nail your fears to the deck
push off

paddle
until you see
there is no river
there is no boat

I laugh
I cry
I'm the bird
I'm the beak

I am
I am

I went searching for you
lost in the quest
and there
I found myself

you and I
fell in love
there is no two

a game
a game
a game

just love yourself,
accept it all as it is

shoulder is me
head is me
One zero eight nine

stop the play, oh love
enough shapes, enough noise
let's go home
and this is home,
welcome home

The non-dual map of 1089:

- Reverse your viewpoint. Flip ego-based perception—just as you reverse the digits.

- Subtract identifications. Let go of attachments and aversions—just as you subtract.

- Add the mirrored Self. Bring in witness-consciousness—just as you reverse again and add.

No matter how far you stray in form, the symmetry of 9 always draws you back to wholeness.
The reversal (1089 ↔ 9801) and the sum $1 + 0 + 8 + 9$ show that

every play of duality—form and emptiness, self and other—collapses into the One.

1089: Any sense of "me versus you" always melts back into "I am."

The Paradox and the Field

1. Align the Body:

Start with the body. When it's open and grounded, the mind clears.
Use tools like chiropractic, acupuncture, or hijama.
Let the spine rise, the breath settle.
Thoughts begin to loosen. Confusion is just movement. Let it move.

2. Soften the Eyes:

Take off your glasses. Soften your gaze.
Stop trying to label everything.

Watch thoughts like birds passing in the sky.
Don't follow them. Just let them be.

3. Listen into Space:

Let sound open you. A bell, a handpan, not music, but space unfolding.
Let vibration dissolve the edges of thought.
Eventually, there's no observer, no thinker, only the field itself.

Don't name it. Don't hold it. Just rest.
Effortless. Spacious. Complete.

> "Since everything is but an apparition, having nothing to do with good or bad, acceptance or rejection, one may well burst out in laughter."
>
> — Longchenpa

You don't need to fix yourself. Just be.
Let body align, eyes soften, sound open.
No inside, no outside. No more chase.
The paradox isn't the problem, it's the proof that you're already free.

The Three Poisons: Letting the Mind Clear Itself

In Buddhism, three poisons cloud the mind: craving, aversion, and confusion.
They're not sins. They're just habits of mis-seeing.
Like dust on a mirror, they hide what's already clear.
You don't need to fight them. Just notice them. And let them dissolve.

1. Craving – Wanting what isn't here.

Always reaching, needing more, never resting.
But the more you chase, the more you forget: nothing is missing.

Let the grasping soften.
Rest in the moment.
Desire rises and falls in space. Just watch.

2. Aversion – Pushing away what is.

Judgment, blame, inner war.
Trying to resist life keeps you stuck in it.

Let anger rise and dissolve.
Even fire is just a dance in the sky.
No need to shrink, stay open.

3. Confusion – Forgetting what you are.

Getting lost in thoughts, stories, overthinking.
You feel small, broken, separate. But it's just fog.

Don't fix the fog. See it.
Even confusion is made of light.
Rest in awareness before thought arises.
Just Let It Be

These poisons don't mean something's wrong with you.
They're weather. Not the sky.

Don't fight. Don't fix. Just be aware.
Let them rise, and let them go.

This is Dzogchen: no war, no chase, no project.
Just openness. Just being.

From poison to nectar, not by struggle, but by space.

"When you rest in rigpa, even poison becomes nectar."

Everything Can Be Fuel: The Alchemy of Spaciousness

What we call demons, emotions, or the moon's pull are not enemies, they are energy: raw, vital, untamed. Neither good nor bad in themselves.

The word emotion comes from the Latin emovere—"to move out"—revealing what emotions truly are: currents of force rising from deep within.

The word demon comes from the Greek daimōn—a guiding spirit, an inner force. Originally neutral, it became feared only when misused or misunderstood. Even the moon, long a symbol of madness and shifting moods, generates no light. It only reflects and reshapes what already shines.

The problem is never the feeling itself—it's the tight grip around it.
When we react with fear or grasping, we distort.
But when we remain open, spacious, and at ease, the same force becomes wisdom.

Dzogchen asks for no fight, no fixing.
Let emotions rise. Let the so-called demons dance.
Don't suppress. Don't follow.
Just rest in the open sky of awareness, where all appearances arise and dissolve on their own.
From that clear space, the best response comes without effort.

This is true alchemy:

> "Not turning lead into gold, but realizing the weight was never in the metal—it was in the grasp."

Patañjali reminds us that even Dharana, Dhyana, and Samadhi—deep as they are—remain outside the seedless stillness. They refine the mind but leave behind subtle seeds, quiet impressions that sprout new stories. These seeds are "fried" only when the final veil lifts and spacious awareness shines on its own, without effort or form.

This is the paradox: practice is essential, yet never complete by itself.
Will opens the door.
Grace carries us through.
One without the other moves in circles.

Hold both views.
Like two wings of a single bird, only together do they let you fly.

Oṁ – One Sound, Two Views

> "Oṁ is made of three letters: A, U, and M.
> They stand for the impure body, speech, and mind of an ordinary person,
> and also the pure, awakened body, speech, and mind of a Buddha."

When most of us chant A U M, we feel separate and unsettled.
The body is tense or tired.
Speech wavers between praise and complaint.
The mind leaps from wish to worry.

But for one who is awake, the same sound reveals what has always been whole.
The body is naturally balanced.
Speech becomes clear and kind.
Mind is open, bright, and still.

Both views are true at once. That is the paradox.
Practice is needed, yet the goal has never been outside you.

To work with Oṁ is not to worship it, but to use it as a mirror. Chant it with care: draw out A, then U, then M, and feel the vibration move upward—from chest to throat to skull. After the final hum, there is a silence so brief it's almost missed. Rest in that. That gap is not emptiness, it is a doorway.

While chanting, remember this: "This sound holds both my confusion and my awakening."
Hold both meanings lightly until they cancel each other, like a flame and its shadow disappearing at dawn. Let the sound fade. And when it does, stay with what remains: spacious, silent presence.

So sit upright.
Breathe gently.
Let the whole body become space.

Refuse the noise of the world: endless ads, empty noise, rigid dogmas, that feed on your restlessness.
More things will never be enough.
Power returns the moment you stop reaching and rest in what is already here.

Breathe, Be Spacious.

May every thought burst like a soap bubble in sunlight.
May every outside fear find no place to land.
May your own clear mind shine without strain,
and may your actions rise naturally from that calm, bright space.

So what's going on here?

The paradox is resolving itself.
We begin with single-pointed focus, like a narrow beam drawn toward the third eye.
This sharp attention is necessary at first, just as glasses help us read the fine details of life.
You gather your energy. You align your will. You refine the center.
This is individuation. The path of clarity. Of becoming.

But once the current is strong and the center is awake, it's time to let go.
Take the glasses off. Soften the gaze.
Let awareness spread, effortlessly, naturally.
The current that rose upward now flows outward into spacious being.

Concentration becomes presence.
Doing becomes being.
Form melts into field.

This is the death of the ego: not in its destruction, but in seeing through it.
It becomes transparent. You realize it was never solid to begin with.
You are still here, but no longer grasping.
You no longer stand at the center, you are the centerless whole.

Individuation was the rise.
Spaciousness is the return.

The paradox resolves:
You become fully you, only to realize you were never separate.
The gaze that once aimed… is now the sky.

And all that's left to do
is rest.
And smile.
And let life flow through you.

Fear Not

> See through it. The circle within the
> square, the triangle within the circle—none
> of it was ever separate. The box is illusion.
> The striving is a story. You were always the wlole.
> Tear the veil, not to escape, but to remember:
> the real you was never hurt. You are already home.

Reality is larger than your threat radar, larger than the maze of endless tasks and relentless goals you've built around yourself. It stretches beyond the anxious checking, judging, and racing, a horizon of peace always there, quietly waiting for you to notice.

Step outside. Walk gently into nature's embrace. Feel the earth beneath your feet and breathe the air as though for the first time. Be still. This is the only action truly needed, to pause and remember solitude's wisdom.

Fear not. You are never alone. Life itself supports you. Trust that when you step into silence and nature's quiet rhythm, you'll realize you never want to go back to the frantic chase. Fear fades. Freedom begins.

"Fear not: Reality is larger than your threat radar, and you're not facing it alone. Dance your dance."

The Shift Begins Within

Sometimes, it's not the person who needs to go, it's the version of you that still gives them power.

It's the inner pattern that flinches, the outdated belief that still waits for their approval, or bleeds from their betrayal.

Don't be so quick to exile people.
First, check if what truly needs to leave is your habit of becoming small, reactive, or wounded in their presence.
You can be free without war. You can let go without cutting.
Because true change isn't when they disappear, it's when their hold on your mind does.

The change you seek doesn't begin with others.
It begins within.
And from there, your peace cannot be taken.

There is no shame in trying again and again, in falling and rising, in making mistakes as many times as needed. The Self is never wounded, only the small ego, building castles of pride and fear. See through it.

Shift your thinking. Shift your awareness. Shift your vibration. Think outside the box, the box of fear, identity, and control. Let the triangle vanish, the endless striving, the illusion of becoming. Then pass through the inner circle, the quiet center within. That is the doorway. And when you move through it, not by force, but by surrender, you make the quantum jump. Suddenly, the outer circle is here. It always was. There is no more separation. Only wholeness. Only you, already home.

You are not just a small circle.
You are drawn within the Greater Circle.

The created was never apart from the Creator
for nothing was ever truly created.
All simply is.

The inner and the outer, the seen and unseen,
move as one rhythm, one breath, one mystery.
What limits you is not life,
but the illusion of separation
the illusion of left and right, this and that.

You don't need to escape.
Just quiet within, active without.
That is your freedom.
Isn't that so?

"Dance your dance. Let the noise fade."

Wisdom says, "You are empty."
Love whispers, "You are whole."
Between the silence and the song, my life flows.
Within the W-lol-E, I drop a laugh.
and the cosmos giggles too.

The Treasure House

According to the Tsung Ching Record, when Dazhu arrived at Kiangsi, he informed Mazu that he had come from Yuezhou seeking the Buddhadharma, to which Mazu replied,

"Instead of looking to the treasure house which is your very own, you have left home and gone wandering far away. What for? I have absolutely nothing here at all. What is this Buddha-Dharma that you seek?"

When Dazhu inquired as to the meaning of his own treasure house, Mazu said:

"That which asked the question is your treasure house. It contains absolutely everything you need and lacks nothing at all. It is there for you to use freely, so why this vain search for something outside yourself?"

At these words, Dazhu experienced enlightenment. He later said of this encounter with Mazu:

"I, the poor priest, heard that the Reverend in Jiangxi said, 'Your own treasure is perfectly complete; you are free to use it and do not need to seek outside.'

From that moment onward, I have ceased [from my seeking]."

"Just have faith in this thing that is operating in you right now. Outside of it, nothing else exists."

— Linji Yixuan

A Zen master once said:
"What are you looking at me for? I don't have it — you have."

Laugh and adjust to whatever life throws, whether you give it meaning or not is yours to choose, so take that power back; it was always yours.

"Silence within, dance without"

Be inwardly still, but outwardly alive.
Act without attachment. Express without losing your center.
Let your actions rise from peace, not noise.

I am alive.
I am luminous, empty, and full of potential.
And that is enough. I am enough.

The Lokas Within the Mind

Buddhist cosmology names many lokas, from the hell realms to the god realms. These are not external territories; they are projections inside the luminous, spacious mind. When awareness is experienced as whole, each loka appears and dissolves like an image in a clear mirror.

Carl Jung called this wholeness the Self: "The Self is not only the centre but also the circumference … it is the totality of the psyche in all its aspects." Realising the Self is to meet the same open field that Dzogchen calls rigpa, an already-awake clarity that contains samsara and nirvana without being stained by either.

To reach this recognition you do not fight the ego; you see through it, just as you see through every changing phenomenon. The ego has no real continuity. It ripens and falls away like seasonal fruit, while the vast, empty radiance of awareness remains.

Practice sketch:

- Recognise projection: List the six basic lokas (hell-beings, hungry spirits, animals, humans, titans, gods) and notice their moods inside you — rage, craving, instinct, reflection, competition, intoxication. See each as a transient cloud in mind-sky.

- Rest in spacious luminosity: Sit quietly with eyes open. Let thoughts rise and vanish, and feel the boundless interval between them. "In original purity all experience is self-liberated."

- Inquiry: Ask, "Who am I without name, body or thought?" Offer no answer; let the question open space.

- Moment-to-moment choice: Out of that openness choose the next word, gesture or silence. Action now arises from clarity rather than from the reflexes of a loka-state.

- Integration: Keep ordinary life in view. Whether washing dishes or sending an email, return to the sense of emptiness that is simultaneously whole.

"Before Nirvana, breathe in and breathe out.
After Nirvana, breathe in and breathe out."

Zen teachers use this line to show that awakening does not change the outer work of life; it changes the way each moment is met. Chores stay the same, yet the mind that meets them is clear, open and undivided.

We create demons to feed desire,
and gods to purge it.
Across time the masks trade places:
yesterday's god is today's demon,
yesterday's demon becomes a saviour by dawn.
The roles shift; the stage remains the same,
the clear, luminous mind where every drama unfolds.
See through the play.
Rest whole in the seeing.

All phenomena rise, shimmer, and fade
within your own primordial, spacious mind.

To whom would I complain?
To whom would I pray?
To whom would I assign blame?

Only Us.
Only This.
Only One.
Only Emptiness.

All that appears rises and falls in the clear light of awareness.
There is no "other," no separation.

In the manifest realm, a bird can fly only with two wings. One wing is emptiness, silent and brimming with unborn potential. The other wing is interconnection, the compassionate activity that naturally unfolds. Balanced together, they carry being through the open sky.

When a sage, after long inner storms, at last whispers Shivoham ("I am Shiva"), that word becomes the sage's own mantra, the sage's own yantra. It cannot be borrowed, only lived, for if borrowed, it becomes dogma. It is known only in the silence when the ego screams at its own non-existence, when surrender comes and no thought remains.

Let your realization rest in its own knowing. Let the vast sky of mind stay wide and clear, and let every step you take beat with the twin wings of boundless emptiness and boundless care.

Understand that everyone walks a different path, yet all paths lead toward the same.

What is that same?

The unnameable truth.
The clear light of awareness.
Not a place, not a belief.
but the direct experience of being.

The essence of the Guhyasamāja Tantra, and later Dzogchen, is not to fall back into conceptual grasping, but to remain in direct experience, known only by the Self.

Later, it's not even about experience, because experience comes and goes. The path dissolves into knowing. Once known, it cannot be unknown. What doesn't come and doesn't go?

The empty and alive awareness in which all things appear, it has always been here. You don't reach it. You simply stop turning away.

I remember your love,
I remember my love,
I remember our love
I remember… Emptiness.

"Serve others, and all you truly need will unfold. Give love freely, receive love openly, and the well of love within you grows ever deeper."

"Tragedy is an unfinished comedy."

—Joseph Campbell

So let the play complete itself, right now.

Beneath every creed, trauma, and inherited guilt, one silent pulse beats. Structures bury it, dogmas deny it, egos guard it, yet it has never moved. How many generations must circle the same hurt, defending ideas older than memory?

Drop the script. The cycle ends the instant you see through it. Nothing is lost but the dream of division. What remains is laughter without a laugher, rigpa itself, clear, self luminous and timeless.

When every experience wears off, what does not?
The naked, unmade awareness that neither comes nor goes.

Finished, yet never begun.

"I AM Alive."

Only the beautiful experience of life itself, of existence, of I AM.

Human = earth-born mind-breath.
Hu is the primal sound: Atum's first word, the Sufi chant of the One, the Vedic offering into fire, the raw cry of the heart. Man is the thinking mind that shapes fate. Remember: you are soil and starlight. Feel the ground, listen to the breath, speak with care, and offer every thought into the inner flame. Own your shadow, protect the earth, serve your community. Insight without action is only a sign; turn it into deed and you become the message. Silence completes the mantra; in that still point spirit and matter meet. Wake up, Hu-Man.

A HuMan is awareness appearing as form
a wave of consciousness dancing through thought, body, and story.
Not fixed, not separate, but the meeting point of stillness and movement,
of longing and laughter,
of forgetting and remembering.

A HuMan is not the ego, not the past, not the roles
but the clear light behind it all,
learning to see itself again.

> "You are not what you think you are. You are the awareness that holds all appearances. And your true journey is simply to remember that."

HuM…………..

Self

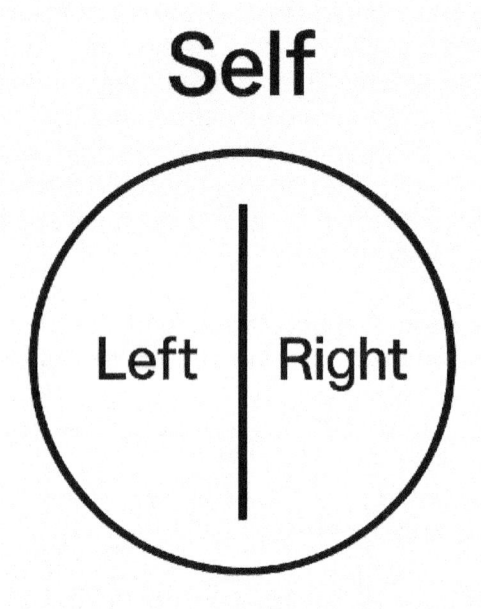

(diagram: circle labeled "Self" divided into "Left" and "Right" halves)

Question: So demons are just sub-conscious systems in your brain? A secular interpretation?

Calling demons "subconscious patterns" may sound secular, yet the story runs deeper.

Hermetic teaching says that All is Mind. Dzogchen lets you meet that Mind before any thought arises. Jung maps how archetypes take shape inside it.

As we begin to uncover the hidden parts of our psyche, once beyond the reach of everyday awareness, those split-off aspects can appear as external beings. It's like climbing a mountain: at each stage, some parts feel unfamiliar, as if they are not you.

But with each step, your awareness widens, and you begin to recognize even the strange and shadowed parts as your own. With every level you climb, you realize they were part of you all along. The gift of this journey is deeper acceptance—and with it, a greater compassion for others, who are each climbing their own mountains too.

As practice widens the view, the picture flips. God is not hidden in you; you arise inside the boundless Mind many call God. The word is only a pointer, for the All cannot be captured by speech.

Seen with more awareness, more spaciousness, these demons reveal themselves as hidden aspects of the ego. The ego itself exists within the psyche, and what is the psyche, if not the soul in motion?

But when the soul awakens to the Infinite, it sees that even it does not truly exist. This is the no-self of Buddhism: not emptiness as absence, but the vast clarity that remains when all illusions dissolve.

When the soul glimpses the endless Divine, it yields and fades, because no one remains to stand apart.

Even the word "One" misleads, because thought still tries to grasp. This is why silence matters, not as escape but as return. The ego here is the limited idea of soul the Stoics warned about, not Freud's functional ego. It is the belief in control and separation.

So be spacious. Breathe. Relax. You do not become something new; you remember what never left.

What about the experiences we have? They arise in the mind. We shape them whether we know it or not. Some bring insight, others confusion. They carry wisdom, yet always with a double edge. That is why they must be interpreted slowly and with care. Their true meaning is often far deeper than what appears on the surface.

It is not to say that experiences should be avoided in the beginning. In the early stages, they are like carrots guiding the donkey forward, glimpses that keep us moving. They hold value, especially when the path is still being discovered.

But as one matures, even these must be released. To dwell on them is to stall. Eventually, one must let go of all clinging, even to the beautiful, in order to rise to subtler planes and witness the play of existence as it truly is.

As the Self, you are the center. And there are as many centers as there are beings, because each one is a doorway to the whole. Even the word "doorway" is loose language. There is no passage, only a veil, and that veil must vanish.

See through the veil. See through your ego. Ask yourself what is here before experience arises, and what remains after it fades. Experience comes and goes. What does not? Every person can realize themselves as the center, not by possession, but by presence.

Empty your mind. Be spacious. Breathe. In stillness we remember our quiet shared power to create whatever we can imagine once we truly know who we are and who we are not.

We are awareness. We are also this temporary world, this brief dance of forms. Do not wait for flowers after death. We are the fruit of this season, and at the same time we are part of That which gives rise to all seasons.

Energy can neither be created nor destroyed. All of this is a play of forms, arising and dissolving, waves moving through the same ocean. Whether we call it God, Awareness, or Consciousness, it is the same essence behind all things. But when we try to name it, we divide it, and from division dogma is born.

So do not name. Do not cling. Feel the Divine. Recognize. Everything is alive.

I AM Alive

Just in the knowing.
Not even knowing
just that which is
before it becomes thought,
before it echoes as "I am,"
before breath turns to word.

No naming.
No claiming.
No asking what it is.

Like the pause between lightning and thunder.
Like the stillness before the seed cracks.

No doorway. No room. Just This.
Unfolding without origin.
Radiant without a source.
Here, always
before every return.

Note: If you're in a transitional period, don't worry, just give it time and let everything settle. Nature always finds its balance, and your psyche will do the same. With that equilibrium come deeper understanding, greater wisdom, and broader knowledge. As Uncle Ben reminds us, "With great power comes great responsibility," and higher wisdom brings its own duties. Meanwhile, a helpful read is "Ego Is the Enemy by Ryan Holiday."

"In my walks, every man I meet is my superior in some way, and in that I learn from him."

— Ralph Waldo Emerson

Look, let me be straight with you: If you can't understand it now, think of it this way, to break one illusion, sometimes you need a greater illusion. And when you finally realize who is holding all these illusions,
all questions dissolve.

Dance your dance. The manifested will catch up later.

Question: If every framework is only a map and reality is always larger than both the subjective and the objective, can I live from a non-dual standpoint and still act in the dual world?

Answer:

- Notice the framework in use and remember it is provisional.

- See that the worrying ego is insubstantial.

- Rest in emptiness, the open field before any split.

- From that silence action arises on its own, clear and effective.

- Language and concepts become tools, not cages.

- Compassion flows naturally because nothing is truly separate.
- Energy once spent defending a self is now free for meaningful creation.
- Move like water, swimming without hooks, ideas, or forms.
- Emptiness is the ground; compassion is the movement.

Common three-part models

Frameworks are just maps. Notice where you stand, then look past the map.

States of mind
- Waking
- Dreaming
- Deep sleep

→ A quiet awareness is present in all three.

Sacred functions
- Creator
- Preserver
- Destroyer

→ A formless presence holds them all.

Body, speech, mind
- Actions
- Words
- Thoughts

→ Pure awareness is the stage on which they appear.

Alchemical principles
- Fire
- Liquid
- Earth

→ An invisible spirit unifies the visible elements.

The hidden "fourth"

Call it silence, stillness, presence, or simple awareness.
Whatever name you give, it remains untouched by naming.

Step through the pattern and stay in the space that was holding everything all along.

The ego that worries about losing a framework was never solid.
Be light, not as brightness but as one who carries no weight.

"Elevate your selfhood to such heights that, before destiny is decreed,
God Himself will ask you, 'Tell me, what is your will?'"

— Allama Iqbal

"Charkha" ("The Spinning-Wheel")
— It belongs to the long Punjabi folk-song cycle called "Charkha" ("The Spinning-Wheel"), sung for at least a century on both sides of Punjab.

O beloved, to catch a glimpse of you
I set my spinning-wheel out in the lane.
People think I spin cotton threads,
but every strand I weave is made of your memory.
My wheel, bright with many colours,
has become the path that carries me to you.
When weariness makes my hands fall idle,
the whir of your remembrance still hums in my heart.
Kin may keep me busy, strangers may stare,
yet the thought of you returns and asks:
"Without you, where else could I possibly go?"

The wonder is that distance was always an illusion. The Beloved is seen the instant the "I" drops away. Let hearts whirl as they will, some spin the wheel of devotion, some trace the razor thread of Advaita's wisdom, others walk the quiet lane of stillness or the busy road of service. Each strand is joy in motion, and every colour dissolves back into what words cannot reach.

"Not a believer in the mosque am I,
Nor a disbeliever with his rites am I.
I am not the pure amongst the impure,
I am neither Moses nor Pharaoh.
Bulleh, I know not who I am.

From first to last, I searched myself.
None other did I succeed in knowing.
Not some great thinker am I.
Who is standing in my shoes, alone?
Bulleh, I know not who I am."

— Bulleh Shah

Dance your dance.
Not the one they taught you,
not the one that pleases the crowd

but the one that rises from your ribs,
spins in your blood,
and forgets the steps halfway through
Simply to remember who you are not.

It is not about finding who you are.
It's about unknowing everything you're not
until you stand as the nameless awareness
beyond all masks.

> "All violence is the result of people tricking themselves into believing that their pain derives from other people and that consequently those people deserve to be punished."
>
> — Marshall B. Rosenberg, Nonviolent Communication: A Language of Life

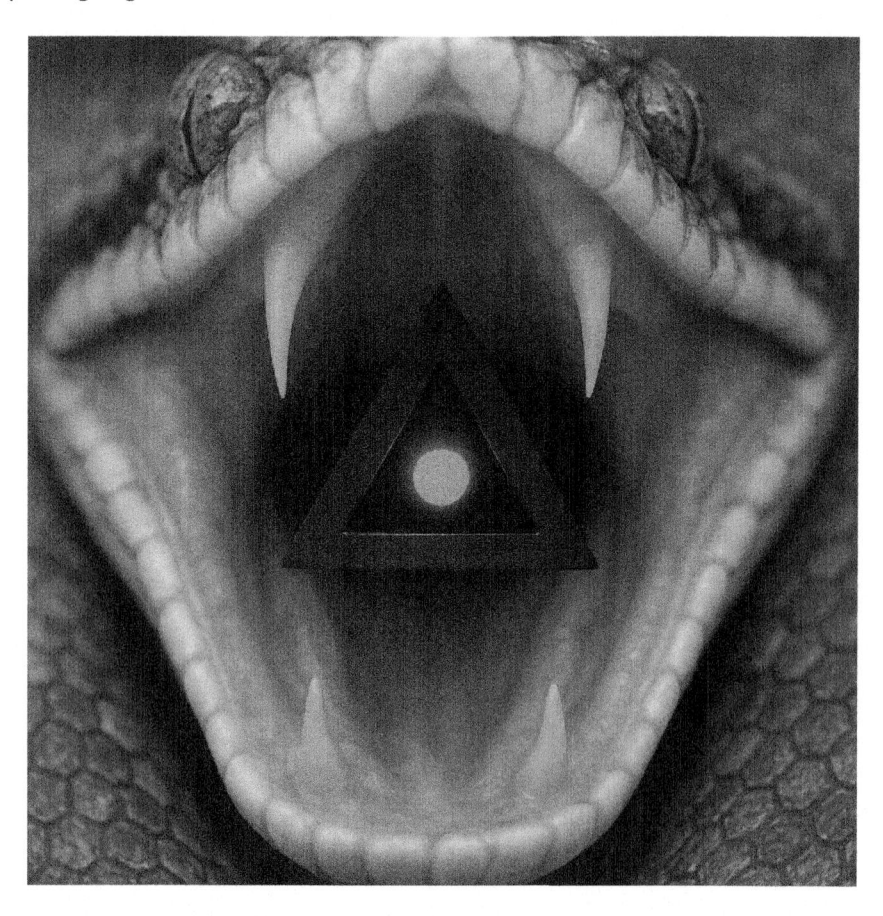

The image is a mandala of self-realisation. It shows that every appearance, from the fiercest instinct to the finest order, is Spirit. When attention rests in the single point, the cycle is seen as play, and action flows from the heart without the need for an intermediary soul.

"Out of this universal feast of death, out of this extremity of fever, kindling the rain-washed evening sky to a fiery glow, may it be that Love one day shall mount?"

—The Magic Mountain, Novel by Thomas Mann

The Fire That Leaves No Witness

In the quiet velvet of a moonlit night a humble fly buzzed toward the mountain palace where the Moth King held court. The fly bowed on trembling legs.

"Your Majesty, grant me the honor of being called a moth. I have wings, I love the night, I too chase brightness."

The King listened, his antennae almost still. "One test will decide," he said. "Whoever discovers the true light first will earn the name."

At dawn the herald gave the signal. Moths poured from the palace in a silver stream; the fly rushed with them, eager and loud. They crossed valleys and orchards until the roofs of a small village glimmered ahead. There, in an open window, a candle burned.

The fly darted close, felt the warm glow on its wings, and sped back to the mountain, announcing triumph.

"I have seen the light, O King. I flew around it and returned. I am the first."

The court grew silent. The Moth King smiled with gentle sorrow.

"The decision was already made," he whispered.

> "The Ego is a veil between humans and God'."
> "In prayer all are equal."
> "Look past your thoughts, so you may
> drink the pure nectar of This Moment."
>
> — Rumi

The final law is simple: emptiness breathing compassion. All forms rise, all forms fall, and every swirl of pleasure or pain is already holy.

So drop the hate, greet every face as your own, and now and then let curious hands wander to dissolve the stiff shell called ego. When nothing is left but warm space, you will see it, the universe smiling, saying, "All is good."

Four Days, No Rewind

Four days. That is all. Step inside and burn the script. When pain knocks, open every pore, let it settle in your marrow, let its fire temper your spine. Hold it without complaint until it melts into a bright river of strength.

When music rises, answer with your whole body. Dance until sweat becomes prayer, until your feet carve stories into the earth. Turn every stone in your soul, stained or pure, and refuse to hide a single shard.

Ask yourself how much agony you can cradle without bitterness and how much joy you can drink without guilt, for both are teachers from the same mysterious source.

There is no encore, no safe return. These four days are the entire stage, and the curtain is already half-drawn. Live so completely that when night falls on the last day, you have nothing left to give and nothing left to regret—only the quiet roar of a heart that tasted everything.

"True mastery is not in chasing extremes but in watching the pendulum swing until you settle into calm balance; such harmony is won only after both extremes have been fully tasted, and that is the jest of life."

Tao Te Ching — Chapter 29

Do you believe you can take over the universe and make it better?
I believe it cannot be done.
The universe is a sacred vessel; it must not be tampered with.
He who meddles with it, mars it.
He who grasps it, loses it.

Therefore the sage,
in the exercise of guidance, does not act with force;
and so the universe flows in harmony.
The universe often runs best under those who do not interfere.

For everything there is a time for moving forward,
and a time for holding back;
a time for deep breath,
and a time for quick breath;
a time to be strong,
and a time to be yielding;
a time to rise,
and a time to fall.

Thus the sage avoids excess, extravagance, and pride.

Freedom from the Known

Truth is simple: a quiet mind.
In stillness the Buddha smiles. Total acceptance flowers. The veil

of ego thins, and the sense of a separate doer fades. Shame and guilt vanish, leaving only the effortless play of a divine instrument.

When the veil is gone the naked radiance of I AM shines. Live lightly. Drop the search. Rest.

If the mind keeps circling, let it. Playing the game is a choice. Watch the spiral, know it as play, and remain free.

It is all here n0w.

"The stars remain faithful to their course; human nature strays, for that is the game, and no one is to blame. Know the moment to stop. Every river finds the sea; all things return to the Tao."

Tao Te Ching — Chapter 48

He who seeks learning will increase every day.
He who seeks the Tao will decrease every day.
He will decrease and continue to decrease
until he arrives at non-doing.
Having arrived at non-doing,
there is nothing which he does not do.

To win the universe, let there be no worldly business.
If one is ever busy, he cannot win the universe.

Breathe in and touch the seventh sky, the unbounded field where nothing wears a name.
Breathe out and return to the first sky, the crisp edge of form.
This pulse of infinity inside limitation is the whole teaching.

Stop hunting for saviours. Each swing from one platform to the next keeps the game alive while the treasure already stands in the spot beneath your feet. Decide now: keep playing hide-and-seek or welcome the raw emptiness that carries every possibility.

No one else can hand you awakening. Every teacher, lover, and politician serves a personal script, knowingly or not. Tear the veil with your own hands. Draw boundaries, break them, draw again, break again, until you remember that freedom is older than every line you trace.

When someone tries to inflate your hope, look at the bones beneath their skin, listen to the noise they make, stay clear.

You, a president, a stray dog, even a pile of refuse, share the same absolute worth and different temporary uses. Accept this, live in vivid sincerity. Snap the chains, shape what you choose, then release it with the next breath.

Tao Te Ching — Chapter 6

The Valley Spirit never dies.
It is named the Mysterious Feminine.
And the doorway of the Mysterious Feminine
is the base from which Heaven and Earth sprang.
It is there within us all the while;
draw upon it as you will, it never runs dry.

"Know enough to realize you don't know. Still, act. Still, create. Still, flow. And in that rhythm, the fourth is felt, not found."

Tao Te Ching — Chapter 32

Tao, in its eternal aspect, is unchanging and has no name.
Though in its primordial simplicity it may be small,
the world dares not claim its possession.
If rulers could abide by it,
all things would be transformed by their presence.

Heaven and earth would unite,
and sweet dew would fall.
People would be righteous
without the enforcement of law.

As soon as Tao is manifested, there is a name.
There are already enough names.
We should know when to stop.
Knowing how to stop
frees one from danger.

Tao in the world
may be compared to rivers and streams
running into the sea.

1. Become Empty to Receive

You can't define or label the Tao. The more you try to control or capture it with thought, the further it slips away. To harness it, **you become like it**—empty, open, undefined. Like water, you take the shape of what is needed.

"Be still. Be silent. Be receptive."

2. Do Without Forcing

To harness Tao is to **rule without domination, act without interference**. You lead not by command but by example. In personal life, this means acting with authenticity, not ambition.

Let go of outcomes. Right action flows from stillness, not strategy.

> "Let life unfold without pushing."

3. Stop Naming, Stop Clinging

The moment you start naming, categorizing, and clinging to identities, you fall into illusion. Tao is whole. Naming divides. To harness Tao, **live in wholeness**, not fragments. Don't overthink. Don't get caught in stories. Let things be.

> "Return to simplicity. See without labels."

4. Know When to Stop

Wisdom lies in restraint. Excess breaks harmony. Knowing when to act, when to rest, when to speak, and when to fall silent is how you move with Tao.

> "Moderation is power. Yielding is strength."

5. Be Like a River

Don't resist the current. Flow with life's natural rhythm. Adapt, bend, move downward with humility. All rivers return to the sea— not by fighting, but by surrendering.

> "Live gently, move deeply, return home."

In essence:

> You do not use the Tao as a tool.
> You live it, become it, create like it.
> Without force, without fear.
> The Tao flows through you
> like breath through the body,
> like a river returning to the sea.

What will you create?
Everything you need is here in this moment. Take the first step.

If you think fish cannot walk, look again.
They walk today.
Evolution never paused.
We rose from the sea.

"Now rise to your Imagination. The higher you rise, the deeper you bow. Be full by being empty. This is the Way."

Section II

The Silent Elephant of the Psyche
Know There is Nothing in Your Hand

Two Big Tasks

"Know there is nothing in your hand, yet act as though everything is in your hand; know there is no right or wrong, yet do what is right for the moment.

Live from the quiet core, free of grasping and fear, and harm finds no entry; every step flows untroubled through life and death alike."

Life gives us two big tasks.

- First, we build an ego so we can work, love, and stand on our own feet.

- Second, we circle back inside to meet the larger Self that has been guiding us all along.

Carl Jung called this return **individuation** and said,

"The privilege of a lifetime is to become who you truly are."

Marie-Louise von Franz explains that the journey usually starts with a wound:

"The actual process of individuation… generally begins with a wounding of the personality."

When the ego feels stuck, it must lean on a hidden organizing center that Jung named the **Self**.

On the way home the Self sends helpers in a set order:

- **Shadow** – the parts of us we pushed away.
- **Anima or Animus** – the inner feminine or masculine that balances us.
- **Wise old figure** – a voice of timeless insight.

Finally we meet the **Self** itself, "bright and dark and yet neither," the sum of conscious and unconscious life. Dreams may picture it as a stone, a world tree, an elephant, or even the Christ.

Individuation is not escape from the world. It is letting the Self flow through the ego so that "the ability to do what one wants to do" (as Jung said of the elephant) serves both personal growth and the wider human story.

Key take-aways for psychological growth

- The elephant at Muladhara stands for grounded power. Harnessing its energy means taming raw instinct so that motivation, memory, and resilience serve conscious aims rather than rule them.

- Domesticated libido is the first step in individuation. When instinct is befriended, it becomes the stable platform on which all higher development rests.

- Ascending toward Vishuddha reveals the world as mind-made image. Recognising that every sensation passes through psychic filters loosens rigid beliefs and opens space for creative response.

- The "airless" quality of Vishuddha warns that pure abstraction can feel disorienting; anchoring in the elephant's steadiness prevents spiritual bypass and keeps the journey embodied.

- In practice, ground yourself with steady breath and simple movement; visualise the elephant whenever you need courage or patience; and notice how each experience can hold a deeper echo beyond its surface facts. This three-step method of grounding, visualising, and reflecting converts archetypal insight into everyday psychological strength.

- Growth begins by stabilising instinct, matures through integrating symbol and thought, and culminates in a viewpoint where inner and outer are recognised as reflections of one living psyche.

> "To the Hindu the elephant functions as the symbol of the domesticated libido, parallel to the image of the horse with us. It means the force of consciousness, the power of will, the ability to do what one wants to do."
>
> —Carl Gustav Jung's, The Psychology of Kundalini Yoga (Lecture 3, 26 October 1932)

Domesticated Libido

Carl Jung called the elephant at the root chakra a sign of **domesticated libido**.

> "It means the force of consciousness, the power of will, the ability to do what one wants to do."

Libido here is not only sexual drive. It is the whole current of life-energy that pushes us to act, create, and relate. When it is "domesticated," a Self-aligned ego channels this power instead of being dragged by it.

How to achieve it

- **Name the impulse**. Notice every surge of excitement, craving, or anger. Label it "energy," not "problem."

- **Ground the body**. Steady breath, firm posture, daily movement. The body is the elephant's stable footing.

- **Set clear aims**. Write one or two concrete goals that matter to you. Channel surplus energy into those tasks only.

- **Contain, then express**. Pause six slow breaths before you speak or click. Use that pause to ask, "Will this serve my aim?"

- **Transmute**. Redirect sexual or aggressive tension into exercise, art, or service. Repetition wires the new pathway.

Link to self-worth

Guided libido becomes visible achievement: finished work, stronger body, kept promises. Each proof of agency whispers, "I can trust myself." Self-worth grows from that evidence, not from praise.

Shield against outside triggers

When energy is yoked to inner purpose, storms outside lose leverage. Markets drop, critics talk, traffic stalls—yet your current keeps moving toward its aim. You respond; you do not react.

> "The Self is the total, timeless man who stands for the mutual integration of conscious and unconscious." — C. G. Jung

The domesticated elephant now uses its trunk, the focused flexible conduit of force, with calm precision: steady, strong, and perfectly aimed.

The Trinity of Inner Transformation

Shiva – Primordial Awareness

Shiva is the silent witness, the wide and formless field that simply notices. It is pure consciousness before thought or movement begins.

Parvati – Dynamic Shakti

Parvati personifies Shakti, the living surge of life that wants to move, feel, and create. This is the creative pulse behind every impulse and emotion.

Ganesha – Purposeful Energy

Born of Shiva and Parvati, Ganesha shows what happens when Shakti is guided by awareness.

- Elephant head: life-force refined into clear intention.

- Human body: that intention put to work in daily action.

- Ganesha is the rebuilt ego that serves awareness instead of resisting it.

"Om Gam Ganapataye Namaha"

The Three Mountains

The Three Mountains: The Autobiography of Samael Aun Weor is a profound esoteric work, combining autobiography with advanced initiatic teachings. It's not a typical life story, it's a symbolic, alchemical map of the soul's journey toward enlightenment.

Samael divides the spiritual path into **three symbolic mountains**, based on his own inner initiations:

First Mountain: Initiation (Psychological Death)

"Sexual pleasure is a legitimate right of the human being."

The disciple begins serious inner work — dissolving the ego, awakening consciousness, and purifying the mind and emotions through initiatic trials.

Key Practices:

- Self-observation to detect the "I" (ego).

- Sexual transmutation between husband and wife without orgasm.

- Daily psychological death (breaking attachments and illusions).

This mountain corresponds to the First Mountain of John the Baptist — preparing the way through repentance and inner purification. The initiate must pass through the esoteric initiations of the Minor and Major Mysteries (often called the Five Initiations of Fire).

The Five Initiations of Fire

The Five Initiations of Fire in Samael Aun Weor's teachings are esoteric stages of inner development that correspond to the creation and awakening of the **solar bodies** (higher spiritual vehicles).

These are achieved through inner purification and sacred alchemy (sexual transmutation with a spouse, without orgasm).

First Initiation of Fire – Physical Body

- Mastery over the physical body.

- Creation of the *solar physical body*.
- The initiate must live with discipline, chastity, and self-observation.

Second Initiation of Fire – Vital Body

- Mastery of vital/etheric energies.
- Creation of the *solar vital body* (seat of health, energy, and memory).
- Refinement of habits and deeper alchemical transmutation.

Third Initiation of Fire – Astral Body

- Mastery over emotions and desires.
- Creation of the *solar astral body* (vehicle for emotional/spiritual experience).
- The initiate learns conscious astral travel and emotional purification.

Fourth Initiation of Fire – Mental Body

- Mastery of the mind and thoughts.
- Creation of the *solar mental body* (vehicle for divine thought).
- The ego's intellectual pride and attachments must be destroyed.

Fifth Initiation of Fire – Causal Body (Body of Will)

- Mastery of will and intention.
- Creation of the *solar causal body* (the soul proper).

- Entry into true discipleship. The initiate now has the right to be called a *Master*.

These are not symbolic or metaphorical in Samael's system — he insists they are real energetic and spiritual developments that can be achieved through inner purification and sexual alchemy within marriage.

After these, one begins the *Second Mountain*, the path of the Passion, Death, and Resurrection of the Inner Christ.

Second Mountain: Resurrection (Mystical Death)

"The sun of truth rises in the human being and illuminates his world when he lifts his mind from the darkness of ignorance and selfishness into the light of wisdom and altruism."

Having dissolved much of the ego and developed inner bodies, the initiate now undergoes a mystical crucifixion and resurrection — a deep, inner Christification.

Key Practices:

- Meditation on the Christic mysteries.
- Facing deep temptations in higher planes.
- Sacrifices for humanity as a path of redemption.

"Only through the path of Christic love can the soul reach Resurrection."

This mountain represents the passion, crucifixion, and resurrection of the Christ within — not as a belief, but as a direct alchemical process. The initiate dies in the higher worlds and is reborn in the Inner Christ.

Third Mountain: Ascension (Glorification)

"It is absurd to go away from the world while searching the Truth because it is in the world and inside the man here and now."

Complete union with the Divine. The soul becomes one with the Logos, capable of guiding others. Here, Samael claims to reach the level of a *Resurrected Master* and receive his divine name.

Key Practices:

- Absolute elimination of all residues of ego (even subtle).

- Total sacrifice for humanity.

- Inner glorification through divine union.

"One must become a Christ to climb the Third Mountain, and this is only possible through supreme love and total annihilation of the ego."

This is the stage of Ascension — beyond individual liberation, the adept becomes a conscious co-worker with the cosmic plan, an active force of compassion in the universe.

Samael speaks in Christian terms but turns them inward. His autobiography is not a simple life story; it is an initiatory chart packed with symbols, visions, and psychological keys—a mystic's inner scripture.

The same pattern appears in every major tradition: language shifts, but the message stays. We are the ones who must lift ourselves.

Like Ganesha, whose ego has matured beyond dependence on father or mother, we take full responsibility for shaping our path. No outside saviour will finish the work for us; the task is ours, here and now.

"Born of Shiva's stillness and Shakti's surge, we inherit Ganesha's task: to forge purpose from power. Heaven and Earth endure because they serve what is greater than themselves; so must we endure by owning every choice.

The Child of the Cosmos learns this above all: no hand but your own writes your story. Choose, act, and shape the stars within."

Tao Te Ching — Chapter 7

Heaven and Earth are eternal.
Why are they eternal?
Because they do not live for themselves;
Therefore they last through all time.

The Sage puts himself last, and finds himself in the foremost place;
he regards his body as accidental, and his body is thereby preserved.

Is it not because he has no personal and private ends,
that therefore such ends are realised?

"Kundalini is the arrow, the heart its target."

The Mirror of Still Waters

The pond is the first gate. Water holds no shape of its own, yet it reflects every shape. It is the unconscious field that carries memories of species and stars. To look into that water is to look into the oldest layer of yourself.

The Linga that Dances

At the center rises the linga. In Sanskrit, *linga* means "mark," the sign of pure, formless awareness. When the stone awakens as a goddess, stillness begins to breathe.

The pillar turns into posture, silence into movement, emptiness into fertility. Shiva stands as the unmoved witness; Shakti moves as the rhythm of becoming. In one body they reveal that consciousness and energy are not two.

To see the goddess inside the pillar is to realize that the ground of being is already creative. The true Self is not a statue; it is poised motion, a dance without a dancer.

The Serpent with the Eagle Beak

Behind her coils the serpent, keeper of deep earth instincts, guardian of the root chakra. Its scales remember the crawl of life emerging from the mud.

Yet its head carries the golden beak of an eagle, hunter of the heavens, symbol of clear mind and far sight. When fang becomes beak, kundalini energy has climbed the spine and opened the eye of vision.

Earth impulse and sky intelligence embrace. Instinct is not repressed; it is refined. Vision is not detached; it is anchored. Serpent-eagle is the marriage of limbic fire and cortical light, the very circuitry of transformation.

The message is intimate: every emotion, every tear, every tide of the psyche is sacred ground for union. Nothing in the feeling body is outside the temple.

In Jungian language the stone linga is the Self, the quiet axis that holds every layer of the psyche. When Shakti rises inside that pillar the conscious ego turns toward the unconscious and listens without fear.

The serpent that climbs the spine completes its journey in an eagle beak, uniting earth instinct with sky-clear vision. At that instant a new presence enters the inner world. Myth names him Ganesha.

Ganesha is the child of perfect union. His elephant head shows perception broadened past old limits, his round body reflects innocence restored, his single broken tusk records the small piece of ego willingly offered so the larger story can be written. Even the restless mouse beneath him now serves purpose.

In psychological terms Ganesha is the freshly integrated Self, joyful, grounded, and creative. He is the evidence that opposites have reconciled. When he appears within your meditation you know the work of individuation has crossed its threshold and a whole new life is ready to begin.

"How much joy can you welcome without guilt, how much pain can you carry without complaint? Burn in the blazing cross, rise reborn, and if your own dreams cannot bloom, make them blossom through others, for every dream belongs to the same heart."

Anchoring Awareness in the Imageless Sea

Primordial awareness is like a boundless ocean of light. It has no edges, no colour, nothing for the everyday mind to hold. Left without a reference, attention drifts into trance or distraction.

Archetypes provide the necessary moorings. They translate vast, invisible forces into shapes the psyche can meet, work with, and eventually release.

Why archetypes matter

Archetypes arise from the collective psyche. Because they are already familiar to the deeper mind, they stabilise attention without forcing it.

A deity, a mandala, or even a simple symbolic figure gathers scattered energies into a single, luminous point. Once collected, those energies can be refined.

Two complementary lenses

- **Devotional lens**: Treat the form as a living presence. Bow, chant its mantra, visualise its radiance. Devotion melts self-centred tension, opening the heart to awe and gratitude.

- **Psychological lens**: Treat the form as your own latent qualities taking shape. Study it, dialogue with it, integrate its strengths. Insight clears blind spots and restores balance.

Using both lenses keeps the path warm and bright. Devotion without insight risks superstition. Insight without devotion risks dryness. Together they form a complete circuit.

Letting go

Clinging turns medicine into poison. After the work is done, release the image back into the ocean of mind. Recognise that it was always a wave of the same water.

The innate Self stands revealed as lucid presence, untouched by arising or dissolving. Archetypes have served their purpose. They remain available as friends, yet their authority is gone. What remains is spacious clarity, able to play with every form while resting in infinite peace.

> "Hold the form until its virtue blooms, then let it sink into the light. The one who sees, the image seen, and the seeing itself are a single, shining sea."

Swimming in Primordial Waters

Esoterically, the number six remains unfinished because we begin counting from one. From that first step, duality unfolds, and the shatkona, the interlocking upward and downward triangles that unite spirit and matter, keeps seeking a seventh point to seal their union. In this view, "All is One," yet that very oneness already hints at the possibility of two and thus invites imbalance.

When we begin from zero, pure fertile emptiness, duality never takes hold. Here, "All is not Two." Balance is not an achievement but the ever-present field in which numbers rise and dissolve. A quiet witness watches this play.

Recognising that witness, we remember our original nature. We learn to swim in primordial waters without clinging to any form and without slipping into confusion.

Better to learn to swim in the primordial waters, calmly and clear-minded, for this cosmic game has no end.

> The task is to break every symbol so the real essence, always present, reveals itself in this moment. In the luminous awareness that has never left, there is no one to worship, no one to call, no names to chant—only Now.
>
> Self the vessel and the potter
> Self the clay from which it's shaped
> Self that drinks from it
> Self that breaks the vessel, letting it flow
>
> —Rumi

Whatever stirs your blood, do it now. Blank pages, silent strings, and untouched stone are begging for the mark of a fearless hand. Ask no timid why, no nervous how. Your pulse is permission, your breath is blessing. Step once and the universe bends to meet your stride. Flow.

Create without guilt, without fear. We forged every cage, we hold every key. See how each life-thread weaves through all the others, how nothing stands alone. Keep the mind clear as a mountain lake, let no ripple feel personal. There is no fixed self here, only the current. You are the divine tool of becoming, and becoming happens in this second.

Wake up, because tomorrow is a ghost. The ego ends each time awareness falls back into stillness. One chance, one stroke, turn it into a masterpiece. Speak raw truth to the narcissist who feeds on pain. Refuse the hate radio, refuse the scripts that promise heaven later while hell grows underfoot. Lift your frequency beyond their static.

Stand naked in honesty. Raise what is broken, cut loose what is rotten. Act with pure authenticity, and the universe will move in harmony with your heart.

Infinite now. Create.

Tao Te Ching — Chapter 10

Can you govern your animal soul,
hold to the One and never depart from it?

Can you throttle your breath,
down to the softness of a little child?
Can you purify your inner vision
till it is without a flaw?

Can you love the people and govern the state
without interfering?
Can you play the female part
in the opening and shutting of the gates of Heaven?
Can you attain to lucidity
of apprehension without action?

To produce things, to rear them,
to rear them without claiming possession of them,
to do the work without taking pride in it,
to be a leader, not a butcher—
this is called hidden Virtue.

Chapter 10 Commentary

- Stay centered in "the Non-duality."
  Hold onto a quiet, balanced state instead of swinging to emotional or mental extremes.

- Watch your breath.
  When you get tense or excited, your breathing turns shallow. Slow, deep breaths cool the fire inside.

- Notice the small changes.
  "Heaven's gates" (birth, death, every little shift) open and close all the time. By staying alert to the small stuff, you're less shocked by big events.

- Polish the inner mirror—without judging.
  Keep consciousness clear, but drop the habit of labeling things good or bad. Judgments cloud your view.

- Practice "not-knowing."
  Real wisdom is humble. When you admit you don't know everything, you stop forcing your opinions on the world.

- Real enlightenment isn't about showing off insight.
  It's not the ego's spotlight; it's the quiet feeling that comes when the ego steps aside.

- See the world as already complete.
  You can chase perfection forever—or relax and recognize the world's natural perfection as it is.

- Hold the question, not the answer.
  Words and fixed answers freeze reality. Staying curious keeps you alive to fresh experience.

- Act without claiming credit ("mysterious virtue").
  Help, guide, and create, but don't demand ownership, gratitude, or control. Let deeds be their own reward.

- Curb endless wanting.
  Desire pushes you to look ahead and miss what's in front of you. Slow down, turn back, and appreciate the present moment.

- Check your motives.
  The purest action comes from enjoying the process itself—not from hunting for thanks, benefit, or authority.

Takeaway: When things change around you, don't panic, force, or resist. Instead, stay grounded, flexible, and open. That's the Taoist way of flowing with reality, not fighting it.

Freedom from the known

- See knowledge as a tool, not a home.
  Ideas help you navigate, yet clinging to them turns the map into a prison.

- Drop the label in the instant it appears.
  When the mind names something—"good, bad, useful, useless"—watch the label rise, then let it fade like breath mist on glass.

- Stay with raw perception.
  Feel the body, hear the sound, sense the air, before thought turns these into stories. This "gap" is already free.

- Trust silent insight.
  Choices still happen, but they emerge from a quiet undercurrent rather than from rehearsed rules.

- Release ownership of experience.
  Pleasant or painful, let each moment pass through without stamping it "mine." Ownership is the hook that ties you to memory.

- Return to the question.
  Any answer eventually stiffens. Keep the question alive—What is this? Who hears?—and mind stays fresh, flexible.

- Rest in unknowing.
  Sit without seeking a result. When thought slows, notice the spacious, alert not-knowing that remains. That space is freedom itself.

"The clear mirror is most luminous when it reflects nothing in particular. Live from that clarity and the journey beyond knowing is already accomplished. Freedom from the known is the doorway to boundless wonder; when the mind releases what it clings to, the infinite steps forward."

Do you see where the journey is leading now? Can you feel the threshold we are crossing?

Everything must be released—every idea, every belief, every piece of knowledge.
Nothing can be held onto.
Deeper and deeper we go,
Until all that remains is this simple truth:
I know nothing.

Let's go, one more time.
We've walked this path for ten thousand cycles.

With the Divine Mother's blessing,
we return not to seek, but to surrender.
All must go, even knowing.
I know nothing.

The known was never the aim.
Love makes no contract.
The river cannot go back—it must merge with the ocean.
Sink to the root, rest in constancy, settle into tranquil stillness.

When psychology, philosophy, and knowledge can no longer carry you beyond, the real work begins.

When deep non-dual meditation, the still awareness of Shiva, holds the space, Shakti, pure energy, is free to dance and purge the splits of the psyche.

Shiva without Shakti is blind stillness; Shakti without Shiva is restless motion. United, they open the way beyond and give birth to the higher consciousness that is Ganesha.

Sometimes the tongue complains, sometimes it praises. Notice which posture lifts your vibration. Energy never dies, it only changes shape. Turn the force behind complaint into the fuel of creation.

On the existential plane the gate is surrender. In daily life the key is spacious action: act from awareness, do not react from habit. Reaction belongs to māyā; deliberate action joins the cosmic play of līlā.

Pain is the furnace that tempers spaciousness. Hold joy and sorrow in the same clear sky and both will ripen you. Use this life to raise the field of human consciousness.

Love more, care more, and speak your truth without guilt. Become so spacious that fear may enter but can find no foothold.

Release the weight of yesterday and the tension of tomorrow. Trust the divine rhythm. The universe is always speaking; listen without ears and the Mother's guidance will flow through every moment.

If you keep only one belief, let it be this: creation blossoms from love, and you are loved without condition.

We create problems and then solve them only to spawn more; place attention where you wish energy to grow. Guard that energy. Move your body, nourish it well, and hold your thoughts like passing clouds—present, yet free to drift.

You are eternally blessed. Do not shrink into survival. Walk creatively, speak creatively, sleep creatively. A role may be fixed, yet excellence is always within reach. Let the ego dissolve into open space. Become the river. Flow.

Law of Return

"What you give, you receive. Intention is the hidden seed. Dance three true steps, and the fourth will unfold on its own. Don't ask how. It just works."

A new cycle has begun. Release the old, welcome the new. This is the moment for fresh starts, new energy, new directions. Walk your path with trust and quiet confidence. The universe is not blind—it moves with those who move with purpose.

Know your target, and your steps will find their rhythm. Set your aim on true Freedom, not escape but fullness, not running away but arriving fully. When the target is clear, the path reveals itself.

Freedom is not a place, it is a state of being. Walk steadily, and you will reach there surely. Reality is perception; what you see depends on where you stand.

243

Truth is not fixed like a stone, it shifts like light through stained glass. Change your angle, and the picture transforms. Judge less, observe more. Beyond perception lies pure awareness, not opinion but presence.

I am truly worthy of my own being. Why should I shy away from myself? Even if the world agrees with me, without harmony within, there is no bliss. What is meant for me will find its way. I do not force. I just flow—and it feels just right.

"Let go of the conditioned mind and transcend into greater realms, where the soul's gem awaits."

In Tibetan Buddhism, Lord Ganesha is honored as **Ganapati** or **Tsog Dag**, a deity who removes obstacles and supports both worldly success and spiritual awakening.

Though originally a Hindu god, Ganesha was integrated into the Vajrayana tradition through early Indian tantric influences.

Over centuries, he took on a distinct role within Tibetan esoteric practices, often appearing in a more wrathful or protective form, aligned with the fierce compassion characteristic of many tantric deities.

Ganapati is revered not only for clearing external hindrances but also for helping practitioners overcome inner blockages—such as ignorance, ego, and spiritual doubt.

His form is powerful and symbolic: the elephant head represents wisdom and memory, while his large belly signifies the ability to digest all experiences, pleasant or painful.

In Tibetan iconography, he may be depicted with multiple arms, holding tantric implements like the vajra, mala, skull-cup, or axe —each reflecting an aspect of spiritual transformation.

He is often included in rituals meant to secure auspicious conditions for practice, protect the integrity of the Dharma, or bring success to undertakings.

Among the Tibetan schools, particularly the Sakya and Gelug, Ganapati is invoked during *tsok* (feast offering) ceremonies and other tantric rites.

While his appearance may vary—sometimes peaceful, sometimes wrathful—the essence remains the same: he is the remover of obstacles and a guardian of the inner path.

This integration of Ganesha into Tibetan Buddhism demonstrates the fluidity and adaptability of sacred symbols across traditions.

It is not merely a borrowing, but a living transformation. In the mandalas of Vajrayana, Ganapati is not held as a fixed external figure, but as a dynamic state of mind. He is no longer just a mythic remover of obstacles—instead, he becomes the very energy of awakened action.

Free from rigid dogma, his presence clears the subtle blocks within the psyche, allowing wisdom to move, to breathe, and to blossom.

Tao Te Ching — chapter 52

The beginning of the universe
is the mother of all things.
Knowing the mother,
we may proceed to know her children.
Knowing the children,

and returning to the mother,
we escape the danger of death.

Keep your mouth shut,
guard the senses,
and life is ever full.
Open your mouth,
always be meddling,
and life is beyond hope.

Seeing the small is insight;
yielding to force is strength.
Using the outer light,
return to insight,
and thereby be preserved from harm.
This is learning constancy.

"The beginning of the universe is the mother of all things."

- Everything arises from a single Source—the Tao.

- This "Mother" is not a person but the mystery from which all life flows.

"Knowing the mother, we may proceed to know her children."

- If you understand the Source, you understand everything that comes from it.

- It's like knowing the roots of a tree—you'll understand the fruit and leaves better.

"Knowing the children, and returning to the mother, we escape the danger of death."

- It's easy to get lost in the details of the world (the "sons"), but don't forget your Source.

- Stay connected to the Tao, and you transcend fear—even fear of death.

"Keep your mouth shut, guard the senses, and life is ever full."

- Don't always talk or seek stimulation.

- Stillness and simplicity open the door to inner richness.

"Open your mouth, always be meddling, and life is beyond hope."

- Constant chatter and busy-ness drain your energy and clarity.

- If you're always outward-focused, you'll feel lost or burned out.

"Seeing the small is insight; yielding to force is strength."

- True wisdom is subtle: it notices little changes, small signs.

- Real strength isn't domination—it's the ability to bend, yield, and flow like water.

"Using the outer light, return to insight, and thereby be preserved from harm."

- Use what you experience in the world to return inward and reflect.

- That return to inner clarity protects you from poor decisions and unnecessary pain.

"This is learning constancy."

- This path—of stillness, yielding, returning—is not a one-time thing.

- It's a steady, ongoing practice. That's the Tao: not a belief, but a way of living.

In essence:
Stay close to your inner source. Be quiet. Observe. Yield. Reflect. Return. And keep doing it.
That's how you find peace in a chaotic world.

> **The world-generating spirit** of the father passes into the manifold of earthly experience through a transforming medium—the mother of the world. She is a personification of the primal element named in the second verse of Genesis, where we read that "the spirit of God moved upon the *face of the waters.*" In the Hindu myth, she is the female figure through whom the Self begot all creatures. More abstractly understood, she is the world-bounding frame: "space, time, and causality"—the shell of the cosmic egg. More abstractly still, she is the lure that moved the Self-brooding Absolute to the act of creation.
>
> —Joseph Campbell, The Hero with a Thousand Faces

As Joseph Campbell explains in *The Hero with a Thousand Faces* (chapter "The Virgin Birth"), myths of creation and renewal often begin with a divine mother and a hero-child who bring new life into the world.

Across many cultures a similar pattern unfolds: the world rises from a vast, silent sea; a divine woman conceives without a partner; and a child-hero struggles into daylight to guide humankind.

These myths carry both a warning and a cure. When selfish rulers or the stubborn "little ego" drag society into confusion, prophets call for new hope. That hope appears through a humble maiden who receives a divine spark—whether the Andean girl touched by the first ray of dawn, Mary greeted by an angel, or Parvati whose devotion wins Shiva's blessing.

Each tale teaches that,

> The world is reborn when humble receptivity meets creative power.

The mother shapes the physical realm, the child-hero breaks through darkness into light, and ordinary people must then shoulder the ongoing task of ordering life.

Creation, redemption, and personal growth are not events locked in the distant past. They are living processes that begin in cosmic mystery, unfold through courage, and ultimately rest in human responsibility.

Taken together, these stories remind us that the world is always being born, that insight emerges through struggle, and that our choices complete what the gods began: they set the stage, then hand the future to us—symbolising both the birth of consciousness and humanity's journey from instinct to awareness.

Question:
Will the heart understand? That we are loved forever, forever forever.

Answer:
Yes. In the quiet flow of stillness, where all things move without force, the heart knows we are loved forever, forever forever.

That is my friend, Mother, Son, Awareness, and the Fourth…
That cannot be named, because it is you becoming.
It is flow. It is bliss. It is joy.
It is experience itself.

And the ending?
Guess what, you are playing all the parts.
The Mother, the Son, the Still Witness, the Rising Flame.
The crushing foot, the cracking shell, the light becoming form.

But the Fourth…
The Fourth is untouched by anger, envy, lust, greed, hate, pride, or fear.
It neither clings nor resists. It simply is.

That is the Fourth.
Beyond the lower ego, beyond the story.
Flowing in all the skies,
unseen yet present,
silent yet alive.

The fire, stolen or gifted, it makes no difference now.
Prometheus may have lit the first spark, but what you do with it is

the real myth.
You are not just the bearer of flame; you are the forge, the ash, the rising blaze.
This fire does not ask permission.
It burns or it creates.
It destroys illusions or builds worlds.
And it waits, for your hand, for your will, for your becoming.

> "So be like the Bodhisattva. Open heart, open mind. Not judging, not clinging. Not the protector of form, but the presence of love. Search, not to find, but to stay open. Keep breaking your own judgments. Keep becoming. And when the fire comes, do not fear it. You are not here to guard the world, but to light it. Unconditional. Awake."

The Bodhisattva archetype tells you that enlightenment is not the end, it's the beginning. The real work is not to escape the world, but to embrace it.

To remain in the burning world, not with attachment, but with a love so vast and steady it becomes stillness itself. The Bodhisattva does not come to fix others. They awaken within them, shoulder to shoulder, heart to heart.

This is the myth that lives in you. Every time you choose understanding over judgment, presence over pride, and service over self, you are walking the Bodhisattva path. It is not supernatural, but supranatural, beyond conditioning, beyond fear, beyond the grasp of ego.

It whispers a deeper calling: Do not merely transcend the world. Enter it. Eyes open, heart bare. And in your presence, help others remember who they truly are.

> "Every pain is a seed of wisdom. Let it ignite you, not consume you. Let it rise as fuel for the ascension of human consciousness."

IMAGINATION, LIFE IS YOUR CREATION

"Live and let live. Learn to tolerate the opinions and behaviors of others, so they may also learn to accept yours. Let your art serve your soul, not the crowd. Don't take the play of maya too seriously—be the leela, be the flow. Imagination is freedom, and life is your creation."

What you want to create begins with imagination.

I imagine…

A world where presence is enough,
where creation flows from stillness,
where love is not a transaction but a way of being.

I want to create clarity in confusion,
poetry in paradox,
and a mirror so clear
you remember who you are
without being told.

Tao Te Ching — Chapter 81

Sincere words are not sweet,
sweet words are not sincere.

The good man does not argue;
he who argues is not good.

Those who know are not learned;
the learned do not know.

The sage hoards nothing.
The more he gives, the more he has.

The Flow of Heaven benefits and does not harm.
The Flow of the sage is to act, not to strive.

Freedom Is Simpler Than You Think

Think of consciousness like this:

Everyday life shows up in three ways – being awake, dreaming while you sleep, and deep, dreamless sleep.

The sages said there is something underneath all three: a silent, watching presence that never comes or goes. They named it **Turiya**, which just means "the fourth," only because it was listed after the other three.

Turiyātita literally means "beyond the fourth." It points to the same silent presence once you stop treating it as a numbered "state."

When you first hear about it, you may feel "I am the witness of waking, dream and sleep."

When even that idea of being a witness drops away, nothing new appears — only the same pure awareness, free of every label. Teachers call this moment "beyond-Turiya" to remind you not to cling to any concept, even the word *Turiya* itself.

Some yoga manuals add an extra step and talk about **five** states: the three ordinary ones, then a deep samādhi they call Turiya, and finally a relaxed, effortless abidance they call Turiyātita.

That map is helpful for meditators, but its end-point is still the same simple reality: your own conscious being, before every thought or experience.

In plain terms: you are the changeless awareness in which all experiences rise and set. Whether you call it Turiya, Turiyātita, Self, or just "I," it is one and the same. The aim is to notice it, rest as it, and drop the need to name it at all.

All the words — "turiya," "turiyātita," "bodhisattva," even "awareness" — are only pointers.
Once they have pointed, you can let them fall away.

What's left?

- simple, open presence

- a natural tenderness toward whatever appears

- no need to judge, fix, or improve the moment

- living from the quiet sense "I am here," with nothing added

That's all. Names aren't required; life itself is already doing the living.

> "As the spider sends forth and draws in its thread,
> as plants grow on the earth,
> as hairs spring from a living person,
> so does everything in the universe arise from the Imperishable."
>
> —Mundaka Upanishad 1.1.7

Like a spider that spins its web from its own substance, moves freely inside it, and then draws the threads back, the imperishable Source extends the universe from itself, expresses through every form, and in time gathers all appearances back into the same silent wholeness.

Rest into what is. Let the urge to reshape the moment dissolve, greeting it with a quiet thank-you. Feel breath arrive and depart, the universe breathing itself through you.

Love unfolds by itself; gratitude ripens without effort. Wherever you stand in space and time, give your best and release it.

No resistance, no fear, no guilt—only the clear current of life. Each instant appears newborn, complete, unwritten. Taste its joy and flow. Blessings, bliss, ah.

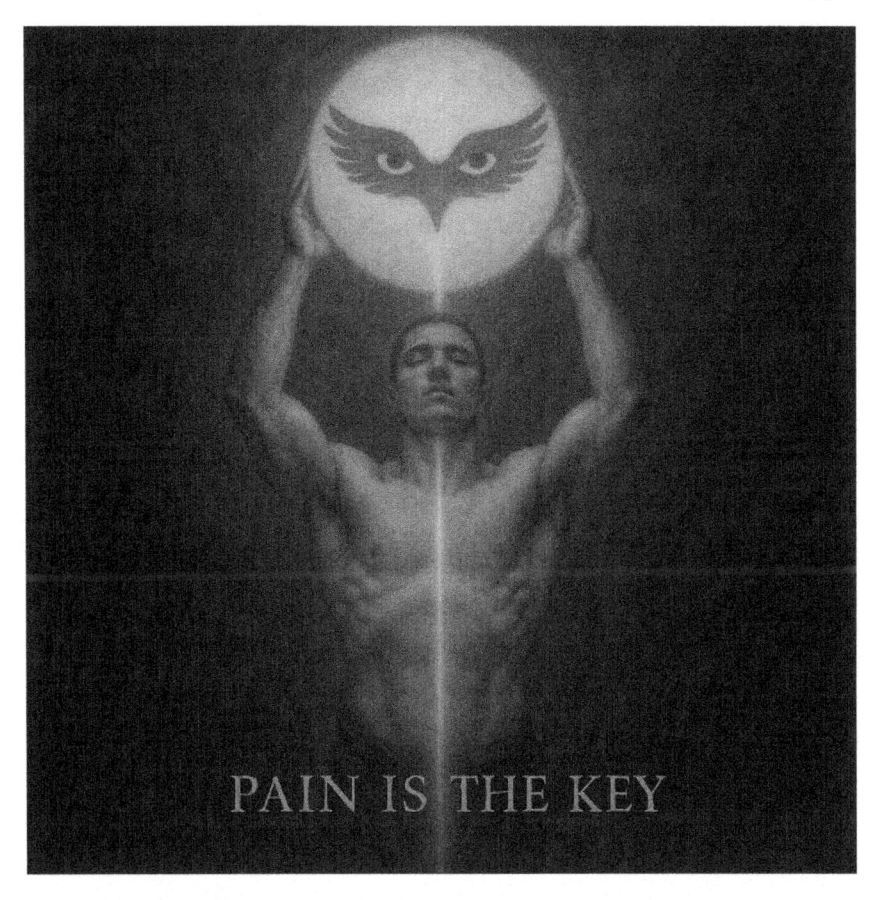

"The journey is not blind. Though the path feels dark and unknown, it moves with unseen clarity. Be the Seer in Flight—one who journeys through the unknown not with fear, but with lucid inner knowing."

The Figure Lifting the Sun

- **Symbol of conscious effort**: The act of lifting the sun represents awakening to inner light, truth, or divinity. It's the soul choosing awareness over unconsciousness.

- **Straining upward = aspiration**: The individual reaches toward their highest potential—spiritual truth, freedom, or realization.

The Sun with the Eye-Winged Eagle

- **The Sun:** Represents the **Self**, **pure consciousness**, **source of life**, and **creative fire** (like Surya, Ra, or Christ-light).

- **The Eye with Wings:** Symbolizes **watchful awareness in motion**—seeing while acting, flowing while perceiving. In esoteric terms, it is the **Seer in Flight**, the awakened soul moving through life with lucid awareness.

- **Eagle Archetype:** Sovereignty, vision, spiritual authority. It connects to solar deities, the Phoenix, and Garuda. It flies highest—closer to Source—yet sees clearly on earth.

Vertical Kundalini Line

- **The central current** (sushumna in yogic terms): The bridge between earth and sky, between the lower self (conditioned identity) and the higher self (spirit).

- **Symbol of inner alignment:** The energy rising reflects balance, awakening, and integration—activating the Spark within.

The Grounded Darkness Below

- Although the darkness and binding forces were softened, they still represent the roots: guilt, fear, conditioning, and ancestral pain.

- The figure rises *not by denying them*, but by anchoring in spaciousness and transmuting those forces into light.

The image embodies the journey of inner alchemy—when awareness anchors in stillness (Tao), the kundalini awakens, and the Seer rises, not to escape life, but to illuminate it. Every knot you open reveal more space, more flow, and more simple joy.

The Tao is not a belief, nor a destination. It is the silent flow behind all things, the space that allows becoming. It does not force, it does not resist. It simply anchors, and in that anchoring, everything transforms.

For the Tao to hold is to allow spaciousness and let the kundalini activate, the living current that can create or destroy, depending on whether the veil of ego is thin and the truth of oneness is recognized.

To be the Tao is to hold space, to be space, not just for joy or clarity, but for pain, confusion, and change. Hold space for growth, both for yourself and for others, for it is the same space.

This anchoring in spaciousness is the deepest offering one can give, and in that openness, things unfold by themselves. If you truly hold that space, you will see there is no one to blame, there is only being.

The more spacious you become, the more the Tao flows through you. You do not chase the Tao. You rest into it. You do not cling to it. You remember you are in it.

Be the Tao. Activate the kundalini.

Look to the sky with clear eyes.
Walk with the strength of the elephant spirit.
Welcome the feminine layers awakening within you.
Welcome the challenge.
Carry your sacred duty with love.
Let your journey unfold in trust and wonder.

> Vakratunda Mahakaya
> Suryakoti Sama Prabha
> Nirvighnam Kuru Me Deva
> Sarva Karyeshu Sarvada

"O Lord with a curved trunk and mighty body, whose radiance is like a million suns, please remove all obstacles in my work, always and in every endeavor."

Om Namo Sri Gajananam
Sri Siddhi Vinayaka Gajananam
Jaya Asta Vinayaka Gajananam
Mangala Mohini Gajananam

"Om, I bow to the revered, elephant-faced Lord Vinayaka, bestower of success and spiritual accomplishment; victory to that elephant-faced One who radiates through the eight sacred forms —embodiment of auspicious grace, draw us ever toward goodness."

Calling Ganesha "Vinayaka" reminds the devotee that every surge of confusion, fear, or delay can be led back into harmonious order. He is the inner executive who turns scattered impulses into clear direction and steady progress.

The eight classical forms of Ganesha trace an inner journey from first awakening to full mastery, mirroring a healthy psychological growth cycle.

- **Moreshwar** marks the moment you feel a clear surge of intention. Like the peacock-riding deity who defeats the first demon, you notice the raw energy that says "begin" and discover courage beneath hesitation.

- **Siddhivinayak** embodies focused competence. Here the awakened intention turns into disciplined practice. You taste self-efficacy, the mindset that effort reliably becomes skill, and your brain starts wiring new success pathways.

- **Ballaleshwar** is devotion expressed as emotional commitment. The trusting child Ballal symbolizes the inner child that wants to love what it does. When passion joins discipline, motivation becomes intrinsic and resilient.

- **Varad Vinayak** teaches receptivity. As you open to life's support systems—mentors, friendships, chance opportunities—

the old scarcity story loosens its grip. Generosity replaces grasping and you learn to ask without shame and to receive without guilt.

- **Chintamani** represents cognitive clarity. Worry, rumination, and mental clutter dissolve as insight sharpens. Mindfulness grows; you see problems before they swell into crises and redirect thought toward constructive solutions.

- **Girijātmaj** is sustained ascent. Like climbing the long stone stair to the cave shrine, you keep showing up when novelty fades. Perseverance becomes habit and scattered efforts fuse into coherent purpose.

- **Vighneśwar** stands for obstacle navigation. Setbacks now elicit curiosity rather than self-pity. You practice emotional regulation, flexible thinking, and creative problem-solving, turning every block into a stepping-stone.

- **Mahāgaṇapati** crowns the cycle with integration. Multiple skills, emotions, and insights align like eight strong arms moving as one. You act from a sense of centered mastery, using your gifts in service to something larger than yourself.

Walk this progression repeatedly and each turn refines intention, skill, devotion, openness, clarity, perseverance, resilience, and integrated action—the living psychology of Ganesha in eight unfolding forms.

Speech cannot grasp the essence; reality is subtler than words. In the playful act of forgetting, the One whispers, "Let me veil my own glory, become many forms, and lose myself in the dance." Thus the play begins.

Even Shiva, in humility, bows to Ganesha, his beloved Son, the blueprint Logos of creation, moved by boundless love. Embrace the universe with the same tenderness you give your child.

- Ganesha is the living intelligence of the universe, the clear mind that turns Shiva's limitless awareness and Shakti's creative force into an ordered world.

- In Western philosophy that guiding mind is called the Logos, the pattern that shapes chaos into cosmos.

- Shiva, Shakti, and Ganesha work as one. Shiva is pure presence, Shakti is dynamic energy, Ganesha is the directing wisdom; together they shine as Sat Chit Ananda, being, consciousness, and bliss.

- Only a small part of the Unmanifest becomes the world we see; the rest stays in reserve as balance. Ganesha decides what crystallises and what remains potential, keeping creation stable.

- The same power lives in every person. Your discriminating mind, or buddhi, is your inner Ganesha. With it you build a private universe through thought, feeling, and choice.

- When you act from clarity and goodwill, life turns into a work of art; when anger, jealousy, or hatred rule, the same creative force bends reality into confusion.

- Surrendering to this inner wisdom is a cosmic joke worth laughing at; it frees you from forcing outcomes and lets the deeper order move through you.

In that embrace the triad of Mother, Father, and Son dissolves into one Self, and that Self is you. Om Tat Sat. Sadashiva.

If Ganesha is the living intelligence that shapes boundless potential into an ordered cosmos, then that same guiding mind beats in you as buddhi, your inborn power to imagine, choose, and create.

The moment you recognize this, the focus shifts from outer events to inner capacity. Your reality can stretch only as far as your own openness.

So the real inquiry becomes simple and intimate:

- How much bliss can you allow before your habits shut the door?

- How much steady will can you hold without slipping into force or fatigue?

- How much true freedom can you welcome before fear tightens the reins?

- The answers are not measured by words but by the openness of your heart.

"Now I bind myself to my Son's rules, and who can contain Her? You wish, haha!"

Remember two rules:

- Rough spikes hide a tender heart. Peel gently, and sweetness appears.

- Real sweetness grows when nature is allowed to finish its work. Let patience ripen every gift.

"And ... the beginning of the Start Show."

Leela—the divine play—is never a battle cry. It is simply a trade of places: strength bears the load, humility enjoys the ride, and life turns into a dance where even the smallest step counts. The moment lives on, not in metal, but in each breath and every choice.

Ganesha, the divine, is not riding the mouse but <u>leading</u> it. The higher self is not above the ego but guiding it with compassion. This is the sacred inversion. Power does not dominate. It serves. Wisdom does not withdraw. It pulls the cart of the restless mind with patience.

Read this image in your own life. When your higher nature pulls the ego rather than fights it, your thoughts become lighter, your actions more aligned, your heart more spacious.

Read it on the level of the world. The greatest leaders are those who serve, not those who sit above. The true intelligence of a society emerges when compassion moves forward first and cleverness takes the back seat.

Read it on the scale of the cosmos. The Source, infinite and ungraspable, chooses to enter form, to bear the burden of matter, to carry even the smallest will, like a mouse resting in a golden cart.

Let Ganesha pull, let the mouse relax, and let your own heart recall that true power is service. When the mighty and the meek move together in love, the whole world glides ahead on silent wheels.

> "This is the Leela, the play where God bends low to lift the smallest parts of itself. The same is required of you: as above, so below."

Because in the end, it's a fucking game.

1. Measuring needs a reference.

You can't say a stick is "one metre" unless you decide where zero starts. In the same way, the mind uses many hidden reference points—memories, body signals, social rules—to judge what is big, small, safe, or scary.

2. The mind is a process, not a thing.

No scientist has found a solid lump called "self" inside the skull. Instead, billions of nerve signals rise and fade like waves in the sea. When those waves line up, we feel "I am here." When they fall apart, the sense of "me" gets thin or even disappears for a moment.

3. Biology loads the dice but does not lock the game.

Genes and brain wiring can make a person more likely to feel guilt, fear, or sadness. Yet the brain is plastic—it keeps changing. Medication, talk therapy, exercise, sleep, food, and caring friends can all shift how the wiring fires. It is hard work, but most people can move their average mood and reduce the spikes of pain.

4. Between thoughts there is a tiny gap.

If you watch your mind closely, you notice brief silence between one idea and the next. Meditators train to rest in that gap. Nothing magic hides there; it is simply the brain resetting before the next wave. Even so, touching that quiet can cut rumination and soften stress.

5. An anchor helps you stay steady.

When strong feelings rise, you can place attention on one steady signal. Some use a prayer or a picture of God. Others, who dislike dogma, use breath, heartbeat, or the sense of space around the body. The anchor is not holy by itself; it is a training wheel for attention and safety.

6. The body is the simplest anchor.

Every moment your heart beats, lungs fill, skin warms or cools. Focusing on these raw signals grounds you in real time. It also keeps emotions in the body, where they can rise and fall, instead of turning into endless stories of blame or fear.

7. No fixed self does not mean "nothing matters."

Seeing the self as a changing stream can free you from heavy shame or rigid roles. But you still act and face results. Kind or harmful waves still spread through family, work, and society. Responsibility stays real even without a permanent soul-stone inside you.

8. Benefits and cautions.

Resting in the body or the gap often brings calmer nerves, clearer focus, and more flexibility with life changes. The risk is using silence to dodge real problems, or drifting so far into "no-self" that daily duties fall apart. Balance matters: empty mind when useful, thinking mind when planning or connecting.

9. The practical recipe.

- Pick a simple anchor—breath, heartbeat, or a value you cherish.

- Spend a few minutes each day feeling that anchor and watching thoughts come and go.

- When strong emotion hits, return to the anchor first, then deal with the issue.

- Keep the body healthy: sleep, move, eat well, and stay in honest contact with supportive people.

- Review with a professional if pain stays high; outside eyes catch blind spots.

In plain words: Everything you know appears as moment-by-moment experience—life itself, alive and breathing everywhere you look. There is no hidden captain steering the ship, only patterns that rise, do their job, and sink again. You can learn to notice the quiet between patterns, choose a steady signal for balance, and keep shaping the stream toward less suffering and more meaning.

> "A Buddha must complain, to remain true to life. Speak freely, but don't cling. Act with presence, then release."

Your game — what is it? I ask you again: what is your game?
Play it.
A billion mouths are vomiting noise — what is your vomit?
Vomit within or vomit without.
Vomit above, vomit below.
However it comes — vomit your way.
Don't hold it in. That's the masterpiece.
Vomit your way.
Nature has crafted a unique masterpiece — You.
And no, you're not special — just unique.
There's no after-after, no wish-wash beyond this.
Don't become a continuity of society, brand, country, family,

tradition, trauma, or trend —
unless there's something in it for you. That's selfishness, and that's alright.
But know this: there is no continuity of you.
This is it — for you, as ego.
Life continues. Life flows on.

And after the vomit, comes the itch — that restless, crawling feeling inside. Ahan. If you don't run from it, if you sit in it without flinching, you begin to master the itchiness of existence. That's where the shift happens. God doesn't feel guilty or afraid of its own vomit. Why should you?

Hey, if you're one of the lucky ones — won the nature lottery — don't waste it. Enjoy your life. Live it fully. Not everyone gets the same roll of the dice. Some never got the ticket. Some never even got the breath.

Anything left?
Illusion.
Darkness—illusion.
Light—illusion.
Misery? Not illusion.
Acceptance? Not illusion.
Bliss? Illusion.

The itch—
The itchiness of existence—
That's the key.
Be in it.
Just be
In
It.

Section III

Untying the Inner Knots
The Courage to Feel, the Strength to Act

The Courage to Feel, the Strength to Act

From ancient times, these have held their power through the One:
Heaven, through the One, remains clear.
Earth, through the One, stands firm.
The gods, through the One, receive their strength.
The valley, through the One, becomes full.
All living things, through the One, come alive.
Princes and kings, through the One, become rulers of the world.

It is the One that gives each its nature.

Without it, Heaven would fall apart.
Without it, Earth would crack open.

Without it, the gods would lose their power.
Without it, the valley would run dry.
Without it, life would vanish.
Without it, rulers would fall and lose their place.

Greatness is rooted in humility.
What is high must be built upon what is low.

That is why princes and kings call themselves "orphans," "alone," and "worthless."

Does this not show that humility is the true foundation of excellence?

The highest honour carries no pride.
Do not seek to shine like jade.
Be plain like a stone.

Tao Te Ching — Chapter 39

Every person carries hidden tensions in the mind and body. These tensions feel like tight knots in a rope. They show up as fear, anger, guilt, low self-worth, or old habits we cannot break.

In oriental teachings this bundle of knots is called **karma** or **samskara**. In modern psychology it is simply stored memory and emotion. When the knots pull tight we react by blaming others, blaming ourselves, or feeling stuck.

How many knots I have loosened, yet a few still cling.
Gold rings once praised as beauty have left their mark on my skin.

I keep untying, knot after knot, breath widening in silent relief.
When the final loop falls open, there is no one left to blame.
only clear, living space.

When the old, lower mind starts its tricks like "You're not good enough," "Stay small," "Feed the habit," recognize the con. It isn't fate or some outside enemy. It's your own neural wiring replaying yesterday's survival script. The body tenses, the gut tightens, the story loops. That's a psychological knot.

"The *natural* mind shines like a lamp; greed, hate, and delusion are just passing soot."

Two layers of mind

- **Surface mind:** Thoughts, moods, impulses, the "old ego software" that spins stories. "I'm stuck… they don't respect me… I need a hit of sugar."

- **Luminous mind:** Clear, alert awareness itself—silent, bright, unhurt. The steady knowing that notices those thoughts without getting dragged.

How to *see* the luminous mind

- **Stop, feel, name.** When an ego-game fires up, label it: "Worry story," "Anger movie."

- **Stay with raw sensation.** Let the body's heat, tightness, or buzz be felt without commentary.

- **Notice the knower.** Behind the swirl is a calm witnessing— clear, spacious, present. That's the luminous layer.

Your mind is already light. Defilements are weather. Learn to watch the clouds, and the sky is obvious.

Archetypes as Mirrors of the Deep Mind

When the surface mind is muddied by fear, doubt, or distortion, the deeper mind responds. Archetypes rise like hidden springs, bringing shape, meaning, and direction to the chaos.

Archetypes emerge from the depths of the psyche precisely when the surface mind can no longer guide us. They appear not as fantasies but as inner realities that reshape perception and restore meaning.

> "It seems to me probable that the real nature of the archetype is not capable of being made conscious, that it is transcendent, on which account I call it psychoid."

— Carl Jung, *Collected Works*, Volume 8, Page 417

Jung is saying that the true nature of archetypes cannot be fully grasped or made conscious. They exist beyond ordinary awareness. Archetypes are not mere thoughts or symbolic decorations. They arise from a deeper layer of reality—at once psychological and more than psychological.

Because they do not belong solely to the mind, yet influence it profoundly, Jung called them *psychoid*. This term points to their mysterious nature, existing at the threshold where mind meets matter, where the visible brushes against the invisible.

In essence, archetypes are not our inventions. They shape us. They rise unbidden from beyond thought, touching both soul and world. They are the language of the deep psyche, echoing the rhythms of the collective and the timeless.

> "The psyche is not of today; its ancestry goes back many millions of years. Individual consciousness is only the flower and the fruit of a season, sprung from the perennial rhizome beneath the earth; and it would find itself in better accord with the truth if it took the existence of the rhizome into its calculations. For the root matter is the mother of all things."

— Carl Jung, Collected Works 18, xxv

Jung is reminding us that the psyche is ancient, not a modern invention or just a product of the brain. Our personal consciousness, what we call "me," is like a flower, temporary and seasonal.

But this flower grows from a rhizome, a deep and enduring root system that lies beneath the surface. That rhizome is the collective unconscious, the timeless layer of the psyche that holds ancestral memories, archetypes, and primal forces.

To truly understand ourselves, Jung says we must include this root layer in our awareness. It is not enough to analyze thoughts or behavior at the surface. We must reconnect with the deep source that shapes all life, the "root matter," which he calls the mother of all things.

In short, the psyche is not a new spark. It is a living branch of an eternal root.

Archetypes arise from the luminous mind as skillful means—forms shaped by wisdom and compassion. They are not final truths, but reflections designed to train and refine the deluded mind. When approached with awareness, they serve as sacred mirrors. When their work is done, let them dissolve like dreams returning to the clear light of knowing.

The three protectors and why they matter

Tibetan Buddhism offers a vivid picture of how to loosen these knots. A famous mantra calls on three figures:

"Om Vajrapani Hayagriva Garuda Hum Phat"

Vajrapani – protector of power
Image: a blue being holding a thunderbolt.
Meaning: pure courage that smashes fear and hesitation.
Inside you: the will to face truth instead of avoiding it.

Hayagriva – guardian of truth
Image: a horse head of red or green fire placed above the main figure.
Meaning: fierce compassion that burns lies, sickness, and pride.
Inside you: honest passion that refuses self-deception.

Garuda – spirit of freedom
Image: an eagle-like bird flying above all.
Meaning: clear vision and rapid liberation from heavy energy.
Inside you: the viewpoint that rises above drama and sees the bigger sky.

When these three work together you meet problems with strength, burn away confusion with truth, and then fly free with clarity.

Facing the Naga

Nagas appear as serpent beings in Hindu and Buddhist lore. Psychologically they are the deep unconscious currents of desire and fear. If we pollute the mind with greed or hatred these currents turn toxic and make us restless or ill.

Nagas are the serpents of the unconscious. To confront them is to meet your own karmic knots, your hidden fear, suppressed desire, and unprocessed pain. To pacify the Nagas is to bring light to your inner depths.

They are **neither inherently evil nor inherently good**. They are **powerful elemental spirits**—sometimes symbolic of deep subconscious forces, unawakened desire, or ancestral karma.

If we respect them through sincere practice they become guardians and healers. So a Naga is not evil. It is suppressed energy waiting for proper care.

Within the **Vajrapani-Hayagriva-Garuda** thangka, the Nagas are the very knots.

- **What you see:** Garuda grips the serpent, Vajrapani stands in fire, and Hayagriva's horse-head blazes above.

- **What it means:** The serpents picture the deep, twisted drives of fear, craving, and old hurt. Left unhealed, they coil into illness or sabotage.

Vajrapani supplies raw courage to face the knot. **Hayagriva** brings the fierce truth that melts its poison. **Garuda** then lifts the cleansed energy into clear awareness.

So a Naga isn't evil; it is **suppressed life-force** waiting for care. When the trio works together the knot loosens, the serpent straightens, and that same energy becomes a guardian instead of a threat.

The mantra that brings it together

"Om Vajrapani Hayagriva Garuda Hum Phat"

- **Om** – The universal seed syllable, opening the mantra and aligning with the enlightened body, speech, and mind.

- **Vajrapani** – The wrathful protector and embodiment of the Buddha's power. He holds the vajra (thunderbolt) and destroys delusion and ignorance.

- **Hayagriva** – A horse-headed wrathful deity and manifestation of Avalokiteshvara (compassion). Known for curing diseases, especially those caused by nagas and dark forces.

- **Garuda** – The celestial eagle who conquers snake energies (nagas), poisons, and subtle energetic blockages.

- **Hum** – Hum represents the unshakable and indivisible unity of wisdom, which is understanding emptiness, and method, which is compassionate action. It is the grounded presence within.

- **Phat** – A seed syllable used to cut through obstacles, illusions, and demonic forces instantly.

Purpose of the Mantra:

- Protection from psychic, energetic, and emotional disturbances

- Liberation from naga-related illnesses and subtle poisons

- Awakening of inner strength and clarity

- Cutting through egoic delusion and inner demons

This mantra unites **power (Vajrapani)**, **compassionate wrath (Hayagriva)**, and **visionary freedom (Garuda)**. When chanted with deep intent and visualization, it burns through inner knots. Chanting this mantra while picturing the thangka painting ignites the same qualities within you.

The Tao, kundalini, and holding space

In Taoist language the ultimate reality is the **Tao**. The Tao is not a belief or a distant place. It is the silent flow that allows everything to grow.

When you stop forcing and start allowing, the Tao simply **holds**. This firm but gentle holding is like an **anchor** in the middle of life's storm.

The same idea appears in yoga as **kundalini**. Kundalini is a living current coiled at the base of the spine. When the ego relaxes and spaciousness opens, this current rises.

If the ego curtain is thick the energy can turn sideways into anger or pride. If the curtain is thin the energy creates wisdom and compassion.

Inner knots are real, yet they can loosen. The power of Vajrapani, the fiery truth of Hayagriva, and the soaring freedom of Garuda live inside you as natural qualities of mind.

The mantra calls these forces forth. The Tao holds them in quiet presence. Kundalini supplies the rising energy. When you honour the Nagas—your own psychological knots—and allow this sacred trio to move through you, fear unravels, blame dissolves, and only clear being remains.

Summary

- **Vajrapani** = Power
- **Hayagriva** = Truth
- **Garuda** = Freedom
- **Nagas** = Hidden Energy
- **Hum** = Presence
- **Phat** = Breakthrough

Cut through illusion. Face each karmic knot. Burn away fear and repression. Release hidden energy with conscious, liberating power. Let steady presence ignite the breakthrough.

> "The lower self burns, the higher self soars, and the True Self stands unshaken amid the flames."

Sky and Thunder as One

The journey comes full circle.

Vajrayoginī, the crimson dawn of naked wisdom, slices every illusion, showing that all forms are empty light. When emptiness is clear, fear has nowhere to hide.

Out of that boundless sky rises the blue thunder of Vajrapāṇi—power devoted to service, not domination. Emptiness turns outward as unstoppable compassion, action that harms nothing and helps all.

Feminine and masculine are one unbroken breath:

- **Vajrayoginī** is the inward collapse of every false wall.
- **Vajrapāṇi** is the outward surge of fearless love.

Emptiness is not a bleak void. It is the seamless field where every being inter-is. When you know this, you feel every heart beat inside your own. Compassion is simply honesty in a borderless world.

- **Prajñā (wisdom) — Vajrayoginī**: Deep seeing that finds no solid core, only a shimmering web. "Form is emptiness; emptiness is form." When this wisdom ripens, seer, seeing, and seen blend into clear light.

- **Upāya (method) — Vajrapāṇi**: Skillful means that sparks like lightning. From the sky of wisdom, deeds burst forth—teaching, feeding, protesting, or silently listening—whatever eases pain here and now. Upāya shields the Dharma and breaks obstacles so insight can dawn.

If you rest only in emptiness, the mind can feel like a clear but chilly sky—open, yet without warmth. If you move only in restless effort, your actions become thunder without rain—loud, yet feeding no one.

Buddhist teaching says wisdom and compassion must travel together. When clear seeing joins kind action, the sky gathers gentle clouds and rain falls, cool and life-giving to all.

Final Turn Holding the Center of the Storm

When anger flares the mind whirls like a water spout. Thought hooks thought, each sharper than the last, and you sink into the vortex that provoked you. Stop there. You are not the whirl.

Step one pace back and simply watch the spinning. In that single movement Vajrayoginī's blade flashes, cutting the lie that you and your thoughts are the same.

From that still stance you meet the next challenge: other people's shadows. Parents, bosses, strangers on a screen may project their own knots of fear or cruelty.

Meet their eyes without flinching. Feel the sting, let it pass through, and refuse to tighten. The Nagas cannot coil around your heart when you stand open.

If their words still hook you, a knot remains inside. Turn inward, breathe into the bruise, and allow it to soften. The world acts as an x-ray; anyone who upsets you points to unfinished work.

Now action is needed. This is Vajrapāṇi's moment. From the clear sky of witnessing let the right response arise: a firm boundary, a calm no, or fearless kindness. This is power that serves awakening for everyone involved.

The cycle now turns around:

- See the spin.

- Step back from it.

- Untie the inner knot.

- Act from sky clarity.

Repeat until the whirlpool is nothing but moving water, and the water is nothing but bright space.

When wisdom and method move together like this, no insult sticks, no fear commands, and no knot stays tied for long. The red wisdom sky and the blue thunderbolt share one body, your own. Walk on.

Remembering Totality

- Aham Brahmāsmi — I am Totality.

- Tat tvam asi — You are That.

There is only one indivisible field of consciousness. It is whole, it is aware, and you are that. The prescription is simple: remember you are That. The conclusion is the same: Aham Brahmāsmi, I am Totality. These words cure nothing; they awaken the ancient memory of who you have always been.

They do not heal like medicine. They stir the knowing that one field of awareness looks through every pair of eyes. When that memory opens, the true cure appears by itself.

The cure is compassionate action.

Vajrayoginī is the red sky of wisdom that sees all forms as empty light. Vajrapāṇi is the blue thunderbolt of love that moves to help where pain appears. Two names, one reality: stillness flashing as aid, emptiness flowering as care.

To know you are the whole is to care for the whole. The breath of that care is Vajrapāṇi in motion, and its insight is Vajrayoginī at rest. Words become medicine, hands become shelter, silence becomes permission for another heart to breathe.

Remember you are That: the boundless, luminous emptiness uncovered by Vajrayoginī, where every form is unborn yet vividly alive.

From that same source, let power rise as Vajrapāṇi's fearless skillful means, adaptive compassion that shapes word and action to the unique needs and capacities of each being in every moment.

> "The wisdom of emptiness embodied by Vajrayoginī and the dynamic compassionate action embodied by Vajrapāṇi are sky and thunder, one indivisible reality."

The Psyche, the Flame, and the Infinite

> "Imagination is more important than knowledge. For knowledge is limited to all we now know and understand, while imagination embraces the entire world, and all there ever will be to know and understand."
>
> — Albert Einstein

The psyche is not a machine. It is not your brain. It is not a collection of thoughts, nor a list of traumas and triggers. The psyche is something far older, deeper, and more luminous.

It is the soul in motion, the inner landscape where experience, memory, image, and longing converge into the mystery of being human.

In ancient Greece, psyche meant soul and was pictured as a butterfly, delicate, transformative, and eternal.

In Jungian psychology, it is the totality of the conscious and unconscious—ego, shadow, dreams, symbols, the personal and the collective all woven into one living field.

In *"The Spiritual Problem of Modern Man"* (from *Modern Man in Search of a Soul*), Jung writes:

> "The psyche is a self-regulating system that maintains its equilibrium just as the body does. The psyche is real. It is not a product of the brain."

In CW11, Psychology and Religion, Jung says:

> "The psyche is a world in which the ego is contained."

Also in *Letters, Volume 2*, he writes:

> "It is quite wrong to think that the psyche is identical with the brain or is a mere function of the brain."

In Eastern traditions, it is called the subtle body: manas as mind, buddhi as intelligence, ahamkara as the ego-maker, and chitta as memory, all revolving around the silent witness, the Atman.

In Buddhist thought, the psyche is not a fixed self but a stream of appearances arising in the mirror of awareness. It is like a pattern in water, vivid, impermanent, and beautiful.

The psyche is where the drama unfolds, but it is not the stage itself. The stage is consciousness, the open and boundless presence in which all things appear. Consciousness is not a product of the mind; it is the light by which the mind is seen.

It does not belong to space or time. It simply is. Timeless, formless, and silent. The psyche is the vessel that holds that light, sometimes stained with confusion, sometimes clear with insight, always capable of reflecting the divine.

And beyond even this lies spirit. Not something separate, but the very flame at the center of it all. Spirit is the breath of life, the current that animates both psyche and body.

If the psyche is the lamp, and consciousness the glow, then spirit is the unstruck fire, the source from which both arise. The purpose of the psyche is not to be escaped, but to be refined, made transparent enough for the spirit to shine through.

This is why the psyche holds within it faculties that defy logic and time. Imagination that sees beyond space, intuition that knows without learning, love that touches beyond death.

These are not tricks of a clever brain; they are glimpses of a deeper order. The archetypes we dream, the symbols that move us, the stories that echo across cultures, all speak from the depth of a shared soul, not a private mind.

Science may measure the brain, but the psyche sings. And in that song is longing, myth, madness, poetry, prophecy, grief, and beauty.

It carries the memory of what we are and the possibility of what we may become. It is not an illusion. It is a mirror, a womb, a crucible. A bridge between the finite and the infinite.

Mother and father, red sky and blue thunder, wisdom and method —these appear as two only until you look from the still point within.

Remember you are That, the boundless luminous field where every form flashes into being and melts back into silence. From that same source let compassion rise as fearless skillful action, shaped to each beating heart.

Walk this world as Vajrayoginī at rest, seeing emptiness, and as Vajrapāṇi in motion, serving life. Sky and thunder are one indivisible reality, and it lives through you.

> Time is brief; joy is now.
> Step off the sidelines.
> Forge what you know into action.
> Live it all the way.

Mother → Child → Mother again

To live wisely is to come home to what you already are. Life begins in the quiet presence of the Mother, the still awareness at the heart of everything. We leave that calm center to explore, chasing names, roles, and desires. This outward journey is knowing the Child.

The farther we run, the more scattered we feel. The mind narrows like a laser, slicing life into tiny pieces, and peace slips away.

Clarity returns when we soften our focus and let the broader light fill the view. Grabbing every detail only breeds trouble. Restraint is strength. Silence is emptiness, yet emptiness brims with life; it is the open space where wisdom softly speaks.

Turn back to the Mother. Close a few doors of distraction. Drop the habit of constant judging and comparing. Then action becomes effortless, contentment rises on its own, and you walk through the changing world unharmed.

In the end, the Child longs for the Mother, and the seeker awakens to the stillness that has been here all along.

> When you loosen your grip on endless doing and knowing, and rest in the quiet awareness that was with you before every thought, life looks simpler, feels fuller, and danger has few places to enter.

The Child's long journey was only a dream, a brief spark in the boundless fire of awareness. Every quest, every ripple of joy or sorrow, every shifting mask of identity was the Mother's own play of light.

Now the dream can relax and the play settles into quiet. What remains is presence, vast and radiant. The fire burns without effort, and the Mother holds all forms in her silent embrace.

Let go and close your eyes for a moment. You are not the spark that flickers and fades; you are the flame itself, the unborn source that never left.

No judgment, no fear, no guilt, no right or wrong. Life is a play. Open your eyes and flow. Chop wood, carry water, breathe and walk. Whatever you do, do it with full awareness and enjoy the show consciously. Live free.

> Row, Row, Row Your Boat
> Row, row, row your boat,
> Gently down the stream.
> Merrily, merrily, merrily, merrily,
> Life is but a dream.

You are not the voice in your head. You are not even the dream. You are the dreamer, slowly waking. So rest now into what is. The thoughts may dance. The world may change. But behind it all is that silent awareness, pure, whole, and free.

The psyche is your journey, but not your jail. Let it serve, not rule. Let it open, not trap. Let it be the painted glass through which the light of your being shines.

This is the secret known to sages, mystics, poets, and lovers. You are not the flicker. You are the flame. Not the echo, but the voice. Not the image, but the light behind the eyes. Timeless, vast, and whole.

And from this knowing, live.
Create beauty.
Love deeply.
Break old masks.

Burn false stories.
And become, fully, what you already are.

> "Your soul won't rest until you remember—you are the flame, not the spark; the dreamer, not the dream; the knower, not the knowing. You are the fourth. You are beyond number, beyond name, never born, and never to die."

The ego appears as a spark, momentary and restless, grasping at identity. It believes it is the source, yet it is only a ripple of the deeper flame.

In Vedanta, the ego is a misidentification, a veil placed over the pure awareness of the Self. In Buddhism, it is empty of essence, a fleeting arrangement of causes and conditions. The Tao reveals that true power flows without assertion, and that wholeness moves quietly beneath all form.

From the view of the limited self, life often seems chaotic or unjust. But in the vision of truth—what Advaita calls the Self, what Dzogchen names the Ground, what Taoism describes as the Way—there is only unity.

No separation, no other. The ego does not endure. It arises, plays for a while, and fades. To surrender is not to lose. It is to remember. You are not the spark alone. You are the flame itself. You are the silent, indivisible fire that dances through all things.

> Return often to the Mother, the source of all becoming.
> Return often to silence, where no voice has yet risen.
> Return often to emptiness, untouched by thought or form.
> Return often to awareness, timeless and unborn.

Is it possible for the ego to know itself? Can the mirror reflect itself without distortion? Can a shadow trace its own edge without light?

We often ask whether the ego can become aware of its own selfishness, its fear, its deep hunger for worth and belonging. But how can a mask know the face beneath it? How can the one who hides be the one who sees?

And yet, something happens—something rare. A moment arrives when the mask begins to crack. Not by effort, not by will, but through the weight of life itself. The death of illusions, the failure of control, the silence that follows exhaustion—these open a space.

When ambition exhausts itself and suffering deepens into stillness, the ego begins to see. But it cannot see alone. It requires the presence of something deeper.

A Self that does not judge, does not interfere, but simply watches with unshakable stillness. The ego learns only when it is no longer the one in charge.

Can the ego escape its own torment? Or is that torment not the flaw but the fire? The furnace that softens its rigidity. The pain is not a punishment. It is the refining process. The agony is the very tool through which something greater begins to breathe through us.

The ego burns not because it is evil, but because it resists what it cannot control. It resists surrender. And yet, the burning is a sacred offering—fuel for the transformation of the whole.

When the ego glimpses the true Self, the vast unbroken field of being, it does not surrender easily. It resists. It rebels. It bargains. It plays victim. It plays god. And then it asks for sacrifice—not to give, but to delay.

Like the lamb on the altar, it does not know that it is both the offering and the one clinging to the knife. It drains you even as it fears dying. But beneath its noise lies something fragile. The ego is not a beast. It is a frightened child that learned to survive by pretending to be in control.

Look closely. Beneath the greed, beneath the envy, beneath the pride—there is confusion. There is fear. There is a hunger to belong. It does not know how to be free. It only knows how to cling. The very behaviors we resent in ourselves are the cries of a self trying not to disappear.

In this, the ancient image comes alive. Life does not destroy the ego by violence. It subdues it through rhythm. Through repetition. Through the steady return of truth.

As Shiva dances on the demon, not to kill but to awaken, so does reality press itself into every layer of illusion until only awareness remains. The demon does not scream—it sleeps under the weight of truth. The dance is not anger. It is the pulse of the real.

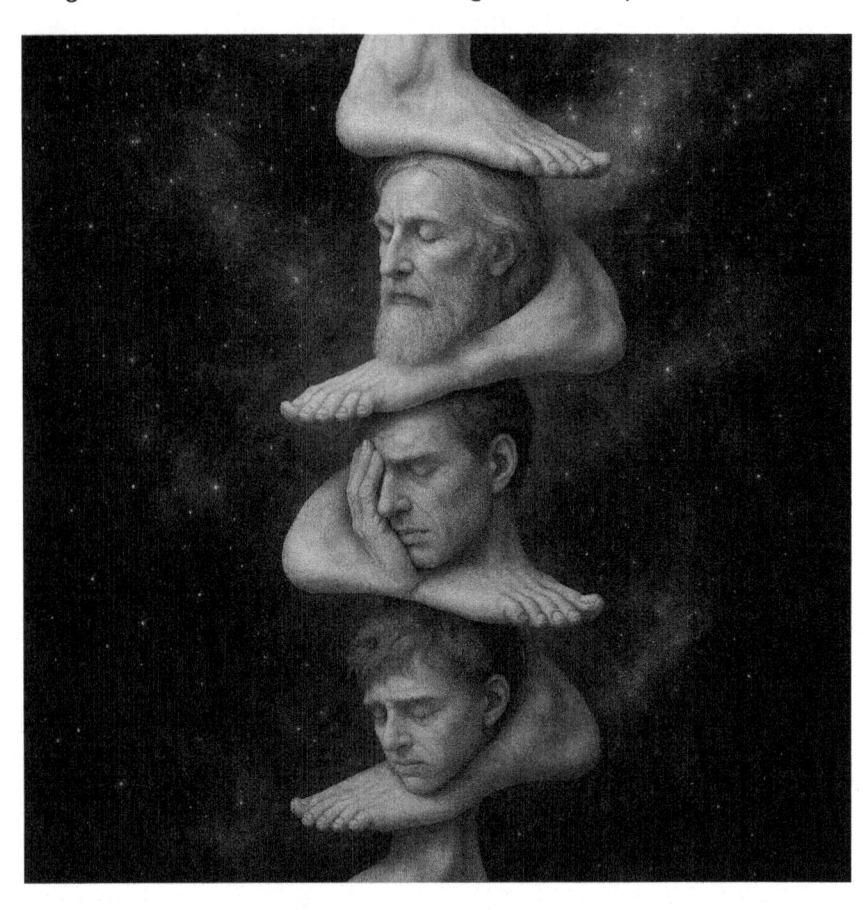

And here lies the mystery. Every ego believes it is the final self until it feels the gravity of something higher. Every self, when seen from above, reveals itself to be just another layer of ego.

What we call growth is simply the loosening of identity, the peeling back of one mask after another. What we call awakening is not a single leap but a continual surrender, layer after layer, identity dissolving into presence.

What we thought was the top was only the next step. What we thought was the end was only the middle.

This pressure from above is not punishment. It is grace—the foot of truth reminding each layer of what it is not. And from below rises the fuel of longing, the fire of suffering that pushes upward to meet it.

Together they create the forge. Grace presses from above, and fire rises from below. Only what is false burns in the meeting place between them. When the illusions fall away, what remains is not light alone, but the union of light and shadow.

Awareness that holds both. Presence that rejects nothing. Not sterile perfection, but living wholeness, where even darkness belongs. No ego, no fixed self, only the ever-turning mystery that reveals itself through contrast.

This is how the ego must be met. Not with a sword, but with compassion. Not with force, but with presence. Be the ground in which it collapses safely. Be the Mother, the space-holder, the still witness.

The ego is not your enemy. It is not your friend. It is a formation—shaped by survival, reinforced by time. The root of suffering is not the ego itself, but the forgetting of what is beyond it.

There is nothing to fight. Nothing to destroy. When remembering returns, the structure begins to loosen. The ego lets go, not by force, but by clarity.

Rest between Yes and No. Between control and collapse. Do not push. Do not pull. The illusion will burn when it must. The truth will rise, not as a thought, but as what has always been.

> "Let it come by itself, by itself, by itself. There is no need to interfere. The psyche reveals itself in stillness, in its own rhythm. Just stay. Just breathe. Just witness. Just flow."

I am everything and I am nothing. Both are true. It all depends on the lens. From one angle, I am the center of my world. From another, I am just a moment in the turning of time.

And from a broader perspective—from far above—you see a vast green meadow, and in it, a single raindrop disappearing into the soil. That too was me. That too mattered.

Is there a God? Is there not? Both answers carry truth. One sees God as the final peak of hierarchy, the grand design above all things.

But when hierarchy dissolves, when we stop looking up and start looking within, we see that divinity does not live only at the top. It lives at the center of everything. Each moment. Each atom. Each one of us.

And with that recognition comes humility. We begin again. We walk differently. We give equal pace to matter and spirit. Because when we grow only in material power, we build weapons. We chase control. We destroy what we fear.

But if we evolve inwardly with the same intensity, those weapons can become fireworks. Symbols of celebration, not domination. Sparks of joy, not war. Explosions of light to mark the end of illusion and the beginning of understanding.

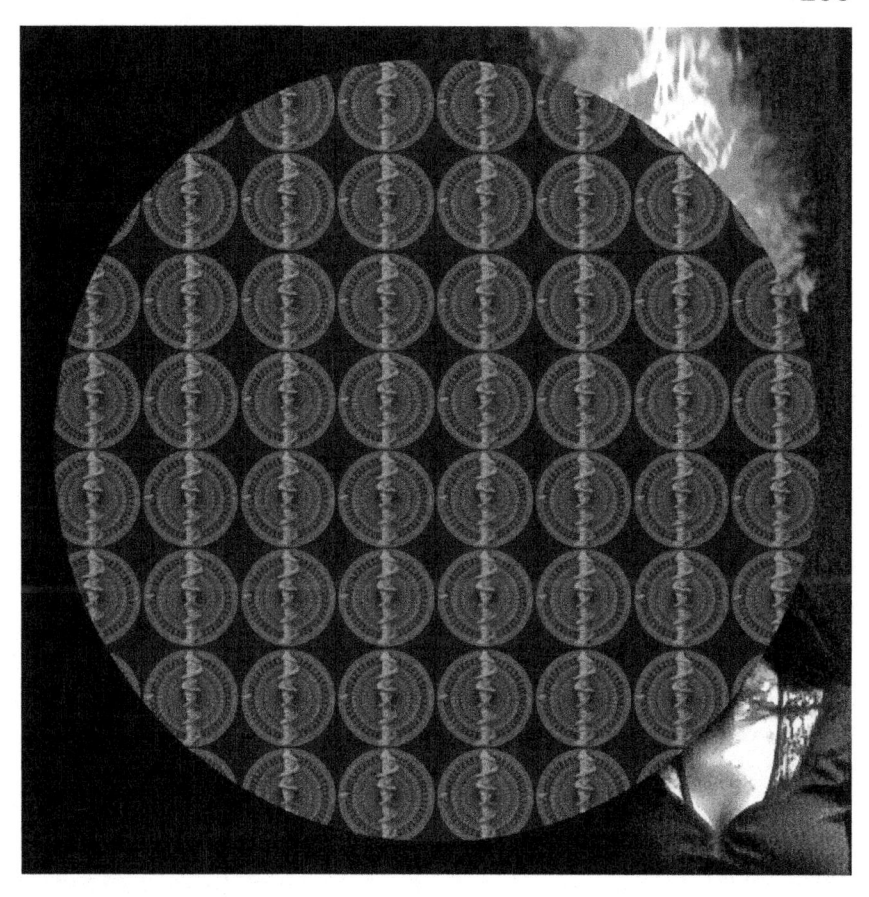

And so, what now?

Sit. Breathe. That's the first step, the last step, the step that was always waiting.

Let meditation be your medicine—not to numb, but to reveal. Not to escape the fire, but to burn rightly in it. Let the smoke of your own illusions choke you if it must, until the air clears, until clarity steps forward, not as a choice but as the only thing left standing.

You do not need to force your way through the dark night of the soul. You only need to sit long enough to see in the dark.

This stillness is not passive. It is revolutionary. Because the mind that no longer reacts becomes a mirror for the world. Because the one who does not flee the inner storm becomes a shelter for others.

Meditation is not only a personal path. It is planetary. A single candle does not erase darkness, but many together shift the atmosphere.

Perhaps that is why, across time and geography, some are called to stillness. To different corners of the Earth. To meditate not only for themselves, but for the whole. To anchor the collective in awareness, so the unconscious doesn't drown the world.

You can join them. You can be one of the quiet ones holding the center, invisible but unshakable. Because in the end, the greatest revolution is not outer conquest, but inner clarity. And sometimes, the most radical act… is to take no action at all.

Just stay. Just breathe. Just be.

The inner universe will move when it's ready. Until then, become the still point. The eye in your own storm. The meeting place of light and shadow.

Be the axis around which clarity turns. Let stillness do what force never could.

> And in that silence, you will remember:
> You were never waiting for the world to change.
> You were waiting to wake from the dream,
> to return to what has always been.
> To stand naked in the now,
> fully here, already whole.

"Any breeze, any leaf, can spark a birth—hero or demon, no one can tell."

Why are you afraid of your own Self? Why are you afraid of your own DNA? From top to bottom, left to right, your entire being is a dancing, wiggly field, a pulsing, vibrating pattern, alive with possibility.

Why fear this wiggliness? Perhaps deep in our subconscious we still carry old jungle fears, the fear of snakes, the fear of what moves, the fear of what cannot be pinned down. But listen carefully: most of this is just a story. And if it is a story, you have the power to awaken from it.

Your so-called "junk DNA," those dormant strands, hold within them the Mother code, the deep creative force, the generative, living field that resides in you. When you activate this Mother DNA, you awaken ancient memory, you reconnect with your intuition, and you open to the subtle vibrations you were born to feel.

But be warned: as you awaken, guilt and fear will arise, not from within you, but from the outside world, from a society that wants to keep you controlled, silent, small. Do not let that stop you. Keep moving. Keep flowing.

The Tao is not rigid. The Tao is the eternal yielding, a flexibility that bends but never breaks. It is the eternal constancy, a quiet, steady return to the source, again and again, no matter the storm.

The world has lost its connection to this living, wiggly energy because of greed, envy, and the hunger for control. But you can reclaim it.

So ask yourself: What are you watching? What are you eating? Are you breathing consciously? Learn to sense your own vibrations. Feel your own stories, not the ones imposed on you.

Feel the Mother within. Emptiness is not absence. Emptiness is pregnant, full, waiting, alive. And it is waiting for you to wake up and dance.

When that particular DNA is activated, you will know it is alive within you. All that is required from you is to remain spacious so you can hold everything from top to bottom and from left to right without guilt, without fear, fully present and open.

> Take care of yourself. Love yourself. Trust the quiet wisdom that lives within you.

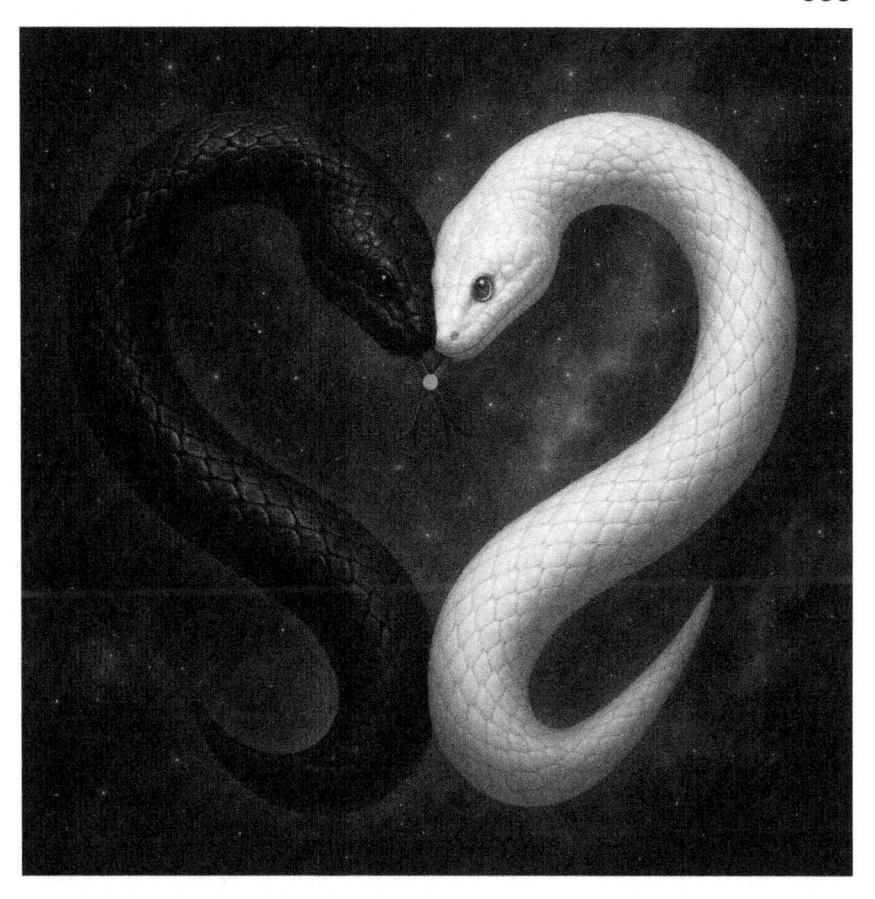

The Tibetan Book of the Dead (Bardo Thodol)

The *Bardo Thodol* is a Tibetan Buddhist guide intended to help a person navigate the states between death and rebirth. It teaches that, after death, consciousness enters the **bardo**—an intermediate realm filled with enlightened and wrathful visions that mirror the mind's own nature.

If these appearances are recognized as projections of the **clear light**, liberation is possible; if not, karma and desire propel the being toward another birth. Traditionally the text is read aloud to the dying or the recently deceased to guide them toward enlightenment or at least a favorable rebirth.

The Six Bardos

- **Kyenay Bardo — the bardo of life**: The entire span from birth to death, our ordinary waking experience.

- **Milam Bardo — the bardo of dreaming**: The dream state, where subtle visions arise each night.

- **Samten Bardo — the bardo of meditation**: Deep meditative absorption in which consciousness turns inward.

- **Chikhai Bardo — the bardo of the moment of death**: The dissolution of the elements and the first flash of clear light as life ends.

- **Chönyid Bardo — the bardo of luminous reality**: Post-death encounters with peaceful and wrathful deities, symbolic displays of one's own mind.

- **Sidpa Bardo — the bardo of becoming (rebirth)**: Karmic winds gather, driving consciousness toward its next embodiment.

Together, these bardos map not only death but the whole cycle of existence, highlighting many points at which freedom can dawn.

Freedom from Attachment

Guilt, fear, shame, craving, anger—none of these are the true enemy. The problem is the clinging that makes them seem solid. Tibetan masters say:

"Thoughts are clouds; mind is the open sky."

Clouds need not be destroyed. See that they were never solid, and you stand in the clear light—timeless awareness beyond every story. Liberation begins not by fighting the mind but by seeing through it.

The Mantra Om Mani Padme Hum

- **Om** — the primal vibration that purifies body, speech, and mind, opening into the unborn quietude.

- **Mani** — the *jewel* of compassionate method, the thunderbolt of skillful action that shatters ignorance.

- **Padme** — the *lotus* of wisdom, unstained by samsara, flowering as the realization of emptiness.

- **Hum** — the indestructible unity of wisdom and compassion, the vajra mind beyond birth and death.

Mani resonates with **Vajrapani** (compassionate power), *Padme* with **Vajrayogini** (naked wisdom). Their union, sealed by *Hum*, is advanced understanding made simple:

> "Be compassionate, act with love, yet know all things are empty —like dreams, reflections, flowing and free."

Beyond God and Self

In the deepest Buddhist view there is no external creator. What exists is:

- **Mind-nature**: pure, luminous, empty.

- **Awareness**: unborn, unceasing, sky-like.

- **Compassion**: the natural outflow when emptiness and interconnection are seen.

Awakening means recognizing this buddha-nature—beyond ego, beyond the very idea of "me" or "God."

Parallels with the Tao

The **Tao** of Daoism is strikingly similar:

- Not a god or ruler, but the nameless source and flow of all things.

- Ungraspable, yet present in every breath—soft, spontaneous, effortless.

> "The Tao gives birth to one, one to two, two to three, and three to the ten-thousand things."

Aligning with the Tao means ceasing force and clinging, letting the way move through you.

> Breathe with the wind, let go of control.
> Stand like the river, whole in each flow.
> Empty your hands, no need to hold.
> Walk as the Tao—silent, and bold.

Sky and Ocean Metaphors

The universal laws are intact; nothing is missing. Clouds may darken the sky, waves may toss the sea, yet:

- The **sky** is never the clouds.

- The **ocean** is more than its waves.

Remembering this is the task: live fully, knowing your nature is wider than every passing storm.

π as a Symbol of Infinity

Pi (π) is the ratio of a circle's circumference to its diameter—an irrational, transcendental number:

π ≈ 3.1415926535… continuing forever without repetition.

See how a silent "0" stands before the leading "3": emptiness first, then the trinity, and from that point the infinite dance begins. Thus π whispers of endlessness—truths sensed but never fully captured, just like the Tao.

Compassion: The Thread We Hold

Since nothing stands alone, let compassion weave us together:

"How can I help you?"

This simple mantra opens hearts, dissolves ego, and turns presence into healing. It is the path of the awakened heart—step by step, lifting one another when we stumble, holding the vision when the road grows dark.

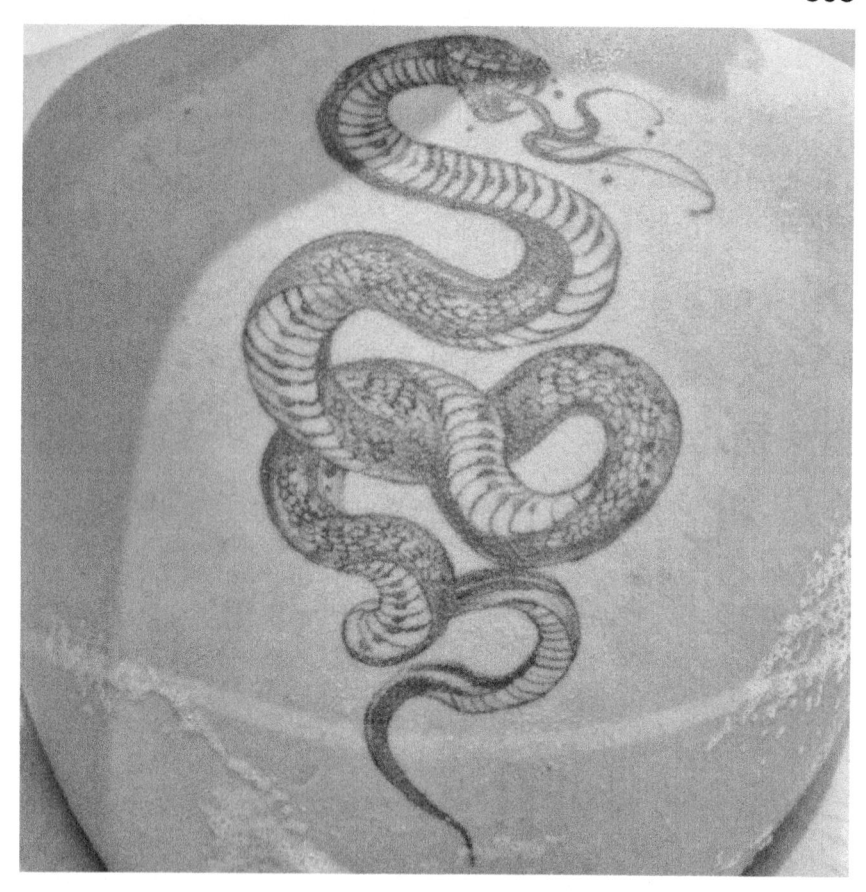

Seeing Others as Ourselves

Ignorance (avidyā) reduces people to objects of lust, power, or use. Awakening reveals emptiness and interdependence, breaking the cycle of craving and suffering. One can no longer treat anyone as "other," for their mind and pain are one's own.

Beyond the Snake: Evolving Past Biology

"To go beyond the snake is to go beyond the limits of biology— beyond hunger, instinct, flesh."

The **snake** is more than raw libido or cold blood; it is a *coil*, a knot of survival drives, traumas, and compulsions twisted tight inside the body-mind. Going beyond the snake is therefore **not** about killing it or fleeing biology. It is about **uncoiling** the knot until its tense spiral becomes a straight, open channel.

Oh Mother, look upon me, see how I have abused you, how I have used you for my small and selfish gain. Oh Mother, forgive me for my shortcomings, for this is who I am, shaped by my limits.

Oh Mother, guide me beyond the serpent's coil, beyond the pull of biology, beyond the walls of my own making. Let me become a pillar of compassion, standing steady in your emptiness.

Oh Mother, surround me as the vast emptiness you are, the boundless space that holds all things. Let me rise through you, for you, as you — whole, humble, and free.

Raw Reflections

- "I need to stop eating meat. Why am I still eating it? Let me start with just once a week."

- "We are not snakes… or are we?"

- "The next stage of evolution lies beyond this body."

- "Perhaps the next evolution is not flesh, but a silicon chip."

- "Beyond the snake means beyond biological limits."

- "To go beyond the snake is to go beyond hunger, instinct, flesh."

- "The dick — symbol of ego and desire — needs to shrink smaller and smaller, until we rise beyond the snake, beyond raw sexual drive, into something freer, vaster, beyond biology."

- "The son must leave the mother's wet womb and step into unknown lands to discover what lies beyond."

- "Let me go, Mother. I must journey to distant lands, toward freedom."

- "Thank you for giving birth to me, but now I need to go far, far beyond — toward more freedom."

Key Reminders

- Be fully present, fully loving; know all is empty, flowing, free.

- Act without forcing, like the Tao.

- Ask, "How can I help you?" — and let compassion guide every deed.

Step by step, heart by heart — we move toward a horizon beyond bone and blood:

past the knots of hunger and fear,
past the coiled snake of instinct,
into a subtler architecture of being,
perhaps circuits of silicon, perhaps bodies of light,
perhaps consciousness free of any shell at all.

Each breath untwists another loop,
each act of compassion codes another lattice of clarity,
until the day the last coil falls away
and we stand upright in the open field.
life-force streaming straight as a beam,
able to choose flesh, chip, or pure radiance as our vessel.

That is where we're going — together.

"The body appears, tires, and fades, yet the life that animates it is love itself — unborn, undying, without limit. Know this, and you live from more than survival; you live from the boundless."

Whether we call the ground of reality "love" depends on what we mean by the word. If we reduce love to emotion or preference, it cannot span galaxies.

But if we use love to name the unbroken intimacy of everything with everything—the fact that atoms bond, stars fuse, minds feel, and beings reach toward one another—then yes: love is a precise pointer.

Physics calls it conservation and interaction; mystics call it boundless presence. Existential philosophers notice the same field from a different angle: in a universe with no predetermined meaning, we are still compelled to care, to choose, to create value.

That caring impulse is love wearing existential clothes. So the cosmic fabric is not sentimental, yet it is profoundly relational. Its very nature is to manifest, connect, and evolve.

Seen that way, love is not an added feature of existence—it is existence tasting itself in every form, from quarks to questions to the tenderness you feel right now.

We have never stepped outside the Mother. We only drifted into layers of dream, each one more detailed than the last. Now we are adding new layers made of code, chips, and augmented worlds.

If we stay asleep, these tools become walls that separate and control. If we wake up, they become bridges that link mind to mind.

To wake up is to remember the Mother as empty, open potential. In that clear space we see that every person, machine, and ecosystem already shares one heartbeat.

Compassion rises on its own, and fear loses its grip. From this clarity we can design systems that heal rather than dominate, guide rather than imprison, and serve rather than exploit.

The task is not to escape the dream but to become lucid within it. A lucid dreamer shapes the story with wisdom and care. When ordinary people recognize their shared root, the next generation of technology can grow like a forest, not a cage.

Equality will follow naturally, because no one will feel separate enough to crave complete control.

Remember the Mother. Feel the quiet in every breath. Let that quiet inform every invention, every policy, every act of daily life.

Then the dream within the dream will unfold as a field of mutual freedom, and each new layer will open wider space for joy.

Owl Headed Dakini

Tibetan: **'ug gDong mKha' 'gro**
'ug = owl ; gDong = face / head ; mKha' 'gro = dakini ("sky goer")

Sanskrit: **Ulūkha-mukha Ḍākinī**
ulūkha = owl • mukha = face

Meet 'ug gDongma

'ug gDongma is a mystical female figure in Tibetan Buddhism, classed as a dakini. She has the head of an owl and stands for deep wisdom that reaches beyond ordinary thinking. She appears in darkness, hinting at hidden truths that shine out when we let rigid beliefs soften.

What She Represents

'ug gDongma shows that real understanding comes when we move past black and white thinking. Her presence invites us to welcome the unknown and find clarity in uncertainty. She helps melt arrogance and strict moralism, leading us toward a kinder and more open view.

In short, 'ug gDongma is a sign of the wisdom that dawns when we release fixed ideas and open to the deeper truths of existence.

$$\pi = \frac{\text{circumference}}{\text{diamater}}$$

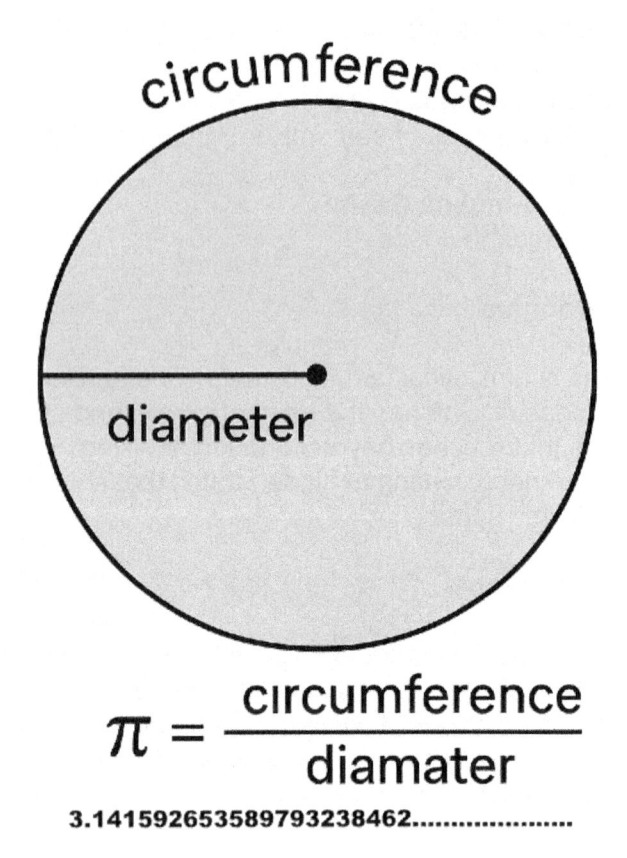

3.141592653589793238462.....................

"Look, you cannot see it; its shape slips away.
Listen, you cannot hear it; it sinks beneath sound.
Reach, you cannot hold it; it slides through the fingers.
These three mysteries blur together and return to one.

When it rises there is no dawn; when it sets there is no dusk.
Boundless and unnamed, it cycles back into nothing.
It is the form of no form, the picture of emptiness, the faint and elusive.

Stand before it and the start is nowhere to be found.
Follow after it and the end cannot be seen.
Rest in the ancient Way, move with the present moment, and you touch the hidden thread that runs through all things."
—Tao Te Ching, Chapter 14

Living the energy of 14 means taking the limitless Spirit of the circle and giving it form in honest words, fair systems, and helpful work. In this way the infinite meets everyday life and turns awareness into compassionate action.

The work is here and now in the material world. The Trinity of Mother, Father, and Son teaches that our higher self must act through our hands, feet, and eyes. Serve, build, and love in this place; that is the mystery made practical.

> "I love science, and it pains me to think that so many are terrified of the subject or feel that choosing science means you cannot also choose compassion, or the arts, or be awed by nature. Science is not meant to cure us of mystery, but to reinvent and reinvigorate it."
>
> — Robert Sapolsky

We must be more compassionate—toward others and ourselves. We must become spacious enough to hold every possibility without shrinking, to see both extremes without collapsing into either.

We need to recognize the place where opposites meet, where the bell curves merge, and feel the mystery that waits there. To stand in the middle is not to be empty, but to touch infinite possibilities.

Each of us is the center of the universe; wherever you stand is your center. And to stand truly at that center, breathe from the heart.

> Let stillness rest between spark and flame, a hush where ideas wait to unfold.
> Breathe that open space; choices spread like wings in newborn light.
> Thought flows on as a clear river, and action follows as a calm sea.
> The pause that joins them beats as the silent heart of the universe.

When you and I are present, without fighting inside, peace is not something we need to search for; it is already here, alive in the simple act of being aware.

You see, it does not matter where we begin; everything finishes in silence, and that silence holds the seed of the next beginning. We just need to go into silence enough times to understand the dance of flow.

And if you ask me what the dance of flow is, it is infinite possibilities, each of us moving through our own dance. But from the still point, in the heart of silence, it is all one flow, one dance, one undivided oneness.

And if you ask me again where this flow comes from, I will tell you, it comes from emptiness, always returning to silence.

And in that silence, we remember we were never separate.

We are all fortunate to have infinite endings and infinite beginnings, each one a gift within the great flow.

> "There is neither creation nor destruction,
> neither destiny nor free will, neither
> path nor achievement.
> This is the final truth."
>
> — Ramana Maharshi

> "Nothing in nature is unclean except when misunderstood. In the presence of the divine, all things are pure. Yet if someone holds something to be impure, then for that person alone, it becomes impure."

Life is play. Silence and play are not opposites; they arise from the same awareness, like waves and calm water sharing one ocean.

Emptiness may seem endless, yet it is never separate from the dance of form. When form appears, tasting it is truth exploring itself. When form dissolves, silence remains and is just as real.

Words such as liberation, enlightenment, and kundalini are also part of this play. They point toward the emptiness already alive within every movement and every pause, but the words themselves are only reflections on the water.

So engage without clinging. Let forms come and go. Friend or foe, joy or sorrow—each ripple travels across the same sea. Witness the play, move within it, and remember that nothing ever departs from the stillness it was born from.

Play is silence in motion. Silence is play at rest. Both reveal the single reality inviting itself to be seen.

Every lack, leak, and tangle of hair shows where the small self clutches at certainty. When you loosen that grip and face the storm of dark feminine power rising within, chaos stops being a threat and becomes a sculptor.

Surrender is the turning key. In accepting life exactly as it arrives, whole or broken, generous or sparse, you discover a grace that cannot be measured, a quiet abundance that flows only through open hands.

With clear eyes lifted to the sky you meet the elephant spirit of steady strength, feel the gentle weight of sacred duty, and welcome the many feminine layers that challenge and refine you. Walk forward in their wisdom.

Let each step marry courage with humility, action with wonder. In this union of surrender and purposeful service the journey reveals its hidden rhythm, and every moment becomes an invitation to live wisdom rather than seek it.

This is the story of Fire Rabbit Ding Mao.

- First, guard your flame: choose people and places that lift your energy, not smother it.

- Second, take the hero's inward path, whether through art, service, study, or prayer, until your inner center wakes and guides your steps.

- Third, master quiet diplomacy: move through the world with alert ears and a still heart, letting calm shape each response.

Remember the Mother, the emptiness shimmering with boundless potential, from which all dreams arise. You and the universe appear together, form and emptiness in one breath. Accept whatever life offers, even what seems lacking, and the dream softens.

If we carry this awareness while shaping new worlds of chips and code, our tools will nurture freedom and connection; if we forget, they will weave tighter cages of control and separation.

Awaken to the quiet emptiness within, and we can dream again together with clear eyes and open hearts.

This is the dance of the Ding Mao fire rabbit, and it is home. Die every night to be reborn anew the next day, that is how Ding Mao beats the spider and embraces the emptiness.

This is your hero's journey, your living myth, your unfolding story. Here and now, in the heart of time and space, you stand at the center of your own stage. Breathe in, feel the pulse of the cosmos within you, and let your next step become a sacred act.

Eat and think only what strengthens your spirit. Say no with calm confidence, knowing that every boundary you set is an embrace of your higher self.

Dance your dance with unapologetic joy, perform your act with clear intent, and don't bother with the echoes of doubt around you.

When you choose what truly nourishes you, the universe moves in rhythm with your courage, and healing rises like a quiet sunrise inside your chest.

Inside this body you stand alone. Whatever you chase, taste, or own, the same untouched space remains within you. Distractions can cloud it for a while, yet when the noise fades you meet yourself again. If you never learn to rest with this aloneness, you miss the heart of life.

See its beauty: no one can enter or take away your inner sky. That clear emptiness is yours alone, wide as the cosmos. Do not fear it. Sit quietly, breathe, and let the silence bloom into joy. In that boundless space you discover that aloneness and wholeness are one and the same.

> "You are not the body. You are not the mind. You are the boundless sky—pure awareness."

This realisation does not ask you to reject the body or the mind; it invites you to embrace every layer of being, the seven skies unfolding within emptiness. The only obstacle is a mind that insists on division.

See that the manifest and the unmanifest are just two faces of one reality, and even those faces dissolve in the open whole. Emptiness dances as form, form rests in emptiness—each level already complete and inseparable.

The lotus and the mud bloom together, inseparable and perfect. Accept the present moment without carving it apart, and the undivided mind shines as freedom.

> Stop before the cup overflows.
> Hone a blade too long, and it goes brittle.
>
> Load a hall with jade and gold; who can guard it?
> Boast of wealth and rank, and you sow your own downfall.
>
> Withdraw when the work is done.
> This is the way of the Universe.
>
> — *Tao Te Ching*, Verse 9

Remember who you are: **Know Thyself**. Then, understand this— the play isn't elsewhere; it's **here, in the manifested**. Don't escape the world. Instead, embrace this profound call to action:

live fully and consciously within the reality that's immediately available.

> "Unmanifest and manifest breathe as the undivided, seamless Now. Embrace this moment and dwell in perfect wholeness. Form and formless flow as one in the eternal present. Welcome the whole, play your part, and witness the flawless Lila unfolding."

You are not going anywhere, nor are you reaching anywhere. You have always been here, and always will be. This is it—the present moment, the creative flow of the Now. Create a new story. Dream a new dream.

> "This is the journey of the Son, born of the Mother and, in the highest realization, one with the Father. Yet in this world the pilgrimage must still be walked by the Father, guided by the Son, and embraced by the Mother within the unfolding Leela, so that, here and now, we may merge into the Absolute."

End where flow begins. Let every teaching be a rung, not a throne. Gather insight from saints, scientists, poets, and skeptics, then fashion an inner compass that keeps turning toward honesty. When any idea grows stiff, breathe out, let it dissolve, and welcome the next current. The mind needs symbols as the body needs food, yet no single symbol can claim the whole sky. Pray to a stone if it steadies your heart, but remember the stone is one note in an endless song.

Let your chosen deity serve as a stepping-stone, then let the stone sink back into the river. The mind needs shapes to grasp, yet each shape is only a pointing finger, never the moon itself. When devotion ripens, the form dissolves into clear space, and you stand where symbols end and the boundless cannot be named.

Feel the pull of non-dual awareness: the quiet sense that the seeker and the sought arise together. Rest there, then step back into the world with clear eyes. When fear whispers of meaninglessness, answer with creative action. When certainty hardens into dogma—atheist or devout—soften it with curiosity.

Keep testing your edges, breaking small limits so larger horizons appear.

Life is not a puzzle to solve but a dance to join. Stand with the simple fact that existence is valuable in itself; all else is commentary. Move, pause, move again. In that rhythm the crisis opens into possibility, and wisdom keeps renewing like water flowing around every stone.

Let every symbol be fertile soil. Draw out its finest qualities—compassion, courage, clarity—and let them bloom in your psyche, shaping thought, word, and deed. Treat each image as a mirror polishing the heart, a seed inspiring creative service, a lamp widening awareness.

Use symbols to expand consciousness, never to attack or divide. Upgrade them when they stiffen, release them when they rule, and let inner silence reveal their deeper meaning. In that quiet space between thoughts, reverence turns toward growth, nourishing life instead of narrowing it. Then symbols unite rather than separate, guiding you to create, to flourish, and to lift every being into an ever widening consciousness.

Bow to the form until it melts into silent space. Then stand within that silence and know: the sheer fact of being is the highest gift. The ultimate treasure is not the symbol, but the simple truth that you are here, aware and alive.

> Die before death; rise anew. Do not miss the chance. Live so fully that each moment is eternity meeting itself.

1. You can't draw a map to the Infinite

- A "map of awakening" sounds neat, but the moment you draw lines you invent two make-believe things: what's inside and what's outside.

- Words can point, yet they can't pin down what has no edges.

2. Talking about Eternity and "God"

- **Positive talk:** "God is love, light, bliss." Nice, but every sweet word drags along its sour opposite.

- **Negative talk:** "God is not this, not that." Helpful for clearing space, yet the idea of "God" still lingers.
- **Simpler option:** drop the whole naming game. The timeless can't fit inside mind-time.

3. The brain isn't built for nonstop bliss

- Your nervous system quickly gets used to any thrill.
- Trying to stay happy 24/7 is like revving an engine all day—it overheats.
- Pleasure spikes are just chemistry; force them and the wiring burns out.

4. What acceptance really means

- It's not giving up; it's living without endless complaint.
- Eat when hungry, sleep when tired. Let the body's built-in wisdom handle the basics; thought can help with taxes and traffic lights, nothing more.

5. Even a rock can be a "temple"

- Gaze steadily at a stone, a tree, or your phone screen. The object doesn't matter.
- Long, choiceless attention melts the felt gap between "me" and "that."

6. Looking for a "way out" is the trap

- The idea that you're stuck and must escape is itself a mental drawing.

- Gate, wall, prisoner—all sketched by thought. Drop the sketch and only life's raw hum remains.

7. Bottom-line conclusion

- **No finish line.** "Enlightenment" is a story thought tells itself.

- **Thought is a tool, not a master.** Use it for practical chores; don't let it run your feelings or invent meaning.

- **Psychological time is a phantom.** Past and future are memory and imagination playing ping-pong.

- **Nothing actually transforms.** Body processes keep ticking; only the chase for "something more" can end.

- **Teachers and techniques are extra luggage.** They promise a trip to a place that exists only on their brochures.

- **What's left is simple aliveness.** Breath, sound, taste—ordinary, immediate, enough.

8. Wholeness and Unity

- Life is already one piece. Thought chops it into "me" and "world," then tries to glue it back.

- The wish to "become whole" creates the very sense of being broken.

- Before labels, every sight, sound, and feeling rise as one undivided field.

- Stop measuring, and unity is obvious.

Nothing to reach, nowhere to arrive. Just this pulse of living, plain and clear, right where you already stand.

Stop decorating the prison.
The bars are thoughts—nothing more than memory flashing through a body that calls itself "me."

"Enlightenment" is a sales pitch.
The body doesn't need it; it already knows how to breathe, digest, and die on time.
It's mind that sells a future payday of bliss so it can keep its rusty gears spinning.

Tear up the map and burn every temple, inside or out.
Then look: no grand silence, no holy light show.
Only the hum of the fridge, the taste of saliva, the weight of your body on the chair.

That ordinary buzz is all there is.
It asks for no applause.
Quit polishing the moment and you'll see the rag, the polisher, and the mirror were never needed.

But smashing every crutch isn't for everyone, and that's okay.
If a candle flame steadies you, light it.
If a mantra, hymn, or sticky note on the fridge clears your head, use it.

Just remember: the power sits in your attention, not in the object.
Rituals and symbols are paintbrushes.
They help you shape the dream until you notice the canvas was always blank.

Wake up to that blank canvas—then keep painting.
Rewrite the scene, remix the tune, tend the garden, raise the kids, laugh, forgive.

Non-duality doesn't cancel the dance; it shows dancer and dance are one ripple.
So hold every practice lightly.
Set it down when it stops serving.

The point isn't to arrive at a final state.
It's to see the game for what it is, play it with a full heart, and keep the play kind.

Feelings pass through us like weather: sun, rain, sun again. We don't have to chase the next mood or cling to the last; just notice the sky changing.

And here's a parting wink for the book:

> I tried to prove I'd finally let go of everything—
> then spent half the afternoon looking for the one sock that vanished in the wash.
> Enlightenment will resume once the laundry's sorted.

Let the storms roll, enjoy the sunshine, and keep playing.

"God of the gaps" is a shorthand used in philosophy of religion and science. It points to a habit: whenever we meet something we cannot yet explain, we plug the hole with the word *God* and stop digging.

Mystery becomes a comfort blanket, and inquiry stalls. In other words, the phrase is not about God at all; it is about how we use a label to avoid the hard work of looking deeper.

Stopping thought altogether is impossible while alive. What we can do is stop clinging to our thoughts as final answers.

A quiet mind is not an empty mind; it is a mind that lets each idea pass through like breath, without grabbing it for safety. From that clarity, action becomes precise rather than reactive.

So the challenge is not to relax into a gap and call it sacred. The challenge is to enter the gap with awake attention and create.

Instead of letting the unknown freeze us or lull us, we treat it as raw space for new possibilities. No shrine, no dogma—only the next step lit by the clean light of not-knowing.

Let the gap remain open. Stand inside it. Then act.

Now begin anew and choose a different play. Why repeat the same drama of enlightenment? The moment you grasp this, you are already free. Congratulations.

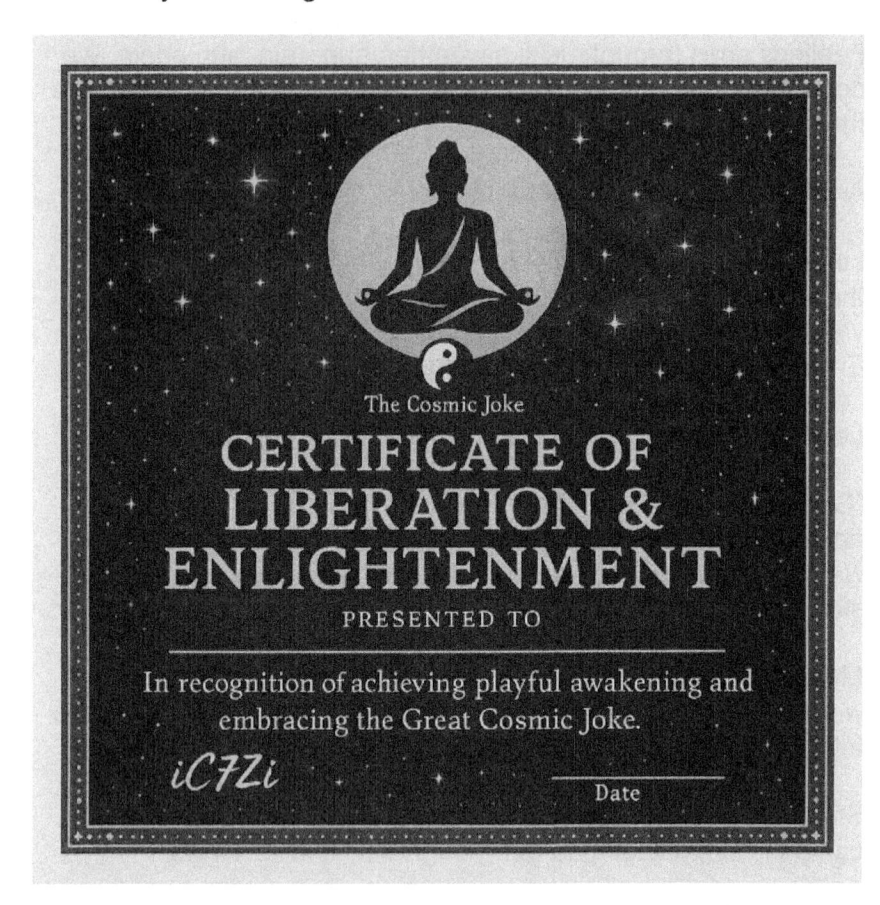

> **The Cosmic Joke**
>
> **CERTIFICATE OF LIBERATION & ENLIGHTENMENT**
>
> PRESENTED TO
> _____
>
> In recognition of achieving playful awakening and embracing the Great Cosmic Joke.
>
> *iC7Zi*   _____
>   Date

"Let us unite to dissolve all suffering, expand consciousness, create with fearless joy, and sail toward untold horizons."

Write your name on the certificate above, and embrace your new life; only you can give this gift to yourself. There's nowhere else to go except right here, right now. I am home.

"The instant you reach for words, the essence slips away.
Just let it go, just be.
You be you, I be me.
In the embrace of emptiness, let us wander, hold each other, and flow as One."

"Let go"

"This is our HOME."

Do yourself a favour: forget everything you have read, toss it on the fire, let the past burn, trade no belief for another, and simply live. When joy comes, taste it; when misery comes, face it; then carry on.

Forget the maps, the prayers, the glitter of high ideas. Dogma is painted dust. Everything you cling to is only a ripple in a dream.

Edgar Allan Poe said, "All that we see or seem is but a dream within a dream." Shakespeare called life "a tale told by an idiot, full of sound and fury, signifying nothing." Take their hints. Thought cannot step outside thought to test its own truth. Every proof is another mirror in a hall of mirrors.

Accept it. All is illusion. There is nowhere to stand that is not already a phantom floor. You will never outrun the haze or harvest perfect bliss. Live in the ache, breathe in the gloom, feel every raw edge, and let the curtain fall when it will.

Forget the writings in this book. All is bullshot. Stop looking for exits. Live in misery, die in misery. That is the naked truth.

Don't worry about old stories—they're just old illusions.
When someone invests too much in an illusion, it becomes nearly impossible to let go,
until another illusion comes along offering even more illusion.
If you accept that *everything* is illusion, there's no need to escape.
The energy wasted in maintaining the illusion of constant bliss is finally released,
and in that release… you *feel*.

So forget old ideas and worn-out tales.
Let's talk about how many robot partners one can have.
Old is dead. New is fire, and then fire becomes old. I think you get the idea.

I AM AN ULTIMATE ILLUSION!

"Any breeze, any leaf, can spark a birth—hero or demon, no one can tell."

People raised within rigid, single-path theologies often find themselves drawn to the vast, many-layered world of Hinduism—with its endless deities, mantras, and yogic methods. After years of confinement, such spiritual plurality feels like oxygen. But every liberating image carries a hidden risk: if held too tightly, it becomes a new cage. The seeker who once bowed to Shiva in freedom may eventually wield his trident to silence others—or worse, to silence their own questioning.

"Let each idea die on time. No shrine left. Just you, alive."

Knowing that every imprint will one day be obsolete grants ferocious freedom. You are always prototyping the next self, fully aware it will also be outgrown. This "death-ground" mindset cuts through perfectionism: ship the project, voice the poem, love the person—then evolve.

Let outdated identities die, making room for a more integrated self. Everything else—scripture, symbol, status—was scaffolding. The building now stands on its own biochemical legs. Walk it into the world.

- Shiva is not a god in the sky. He is the part of you that cuts through illusion.

- Parvati is not a goddess with a name. She is your calm strength and care.

- Ganesha is not a statue. He is your mind solving problems.

You borrowed their names to train those muscles. Now the training is complete. Let them go. If you keep clinging, they become idols. Tribe symbols. Dogma. You'll fight in their name, obey in their name, and get used in their name. The gods don't want worship. They want to be released.

So thank them. Bow once. Blow out the candle. Turn the idol back to clay. Let silence speak where mantras once did. Now show your devotion by living. Cut what's false. Protect what's real. Create what is needed.

- Don't invoke Shiva—*act with clarity.*

- Don't pray to Parvati—*stand with love.*

- Don't call Ganesha—*solve the block.*

This is the final step: not faith, but function. Not belief, but embodiment. Let the Mother go. Let the Father go. Let the Son go. Let them all go. Now live.

Drop the holy trinity. Shiva, Parvati, Ganesha did their job. Courage, care, cunning now live in your nerves. Thank the statues, scrap the altar, walk on.

Drop God too. The question "What is God?" is the questioner talking to itself. When the question falls silent nothing is left to debate.

Drop non-duality. Saying "All is One" or "All is not Two" is still a slogan—another cage with softer walls. Thought cannot outrun thought.

- **Any attempt to escape the mind using the mind fails.** A thought that says, "I'm beyond thought," is still a thought.

- **The 'witness,' mystical insights, even the idea of God are mental products.** They arise in the same stream they claim to transcend.

- **Trying to think your way past thinking just adds another layer.** Like writing "no words" with more words.

So what remains?

- Heartbeat, breath, a crack in the ceiling, the smell of dust.

- A phone that needs charging, a child who needs lunch, a stranger who needs directions.

- Action. Mistake. Repair. Repeat.

- No witness required.

- No ultimate meaning to chase.
- Life moves anyway.
- Let every idea rise, do its work, and die on time.
- Meet the next moment naked.
- That is the only freedom there is.

| Let each idea die on time. No shrine left. Just you, alive.

I know I am—
so the illusion holds.
If anything's left,
I'm still inside it.

No mother.
No father.
No son.
Not even emptiness.

Even rejection is noise.

Take it.
As it is.

Once misery is seen—
not fought—
the rules collapse.

And something moves.
Not toward hope.
Just different.

The great illusionist
gets the biggest share—
not by fact,
but by flare.

He shapes the void,
sells empty light,
and crowds applaud—
too dulled to care.

Play the game,
have your share,
and then—
live in misery,
die in misery.

That's the trick.
That's the flair.

"No more questions. No more answers. There's nothing to know, Bob."

There's nothing to know, Bob.

There's nothing to know, Bob.
The great illusionist

There's nothing to know, Bob.
The great illusionist

"Via Joseph Campbell: My friend Heinrich Zimmer of years ago used to say, "The best things can't be told," because they transcend thought. "The second best are misunderstood," because those are the thoughts that are supposed to refer to that which can't be thought about, and one gets stuck in the thoughts."The third best are what we talk about."

— Heinrich Zimmer

I point you to one thing: your life. No metaphor.
Life is fact, not thought.
Live it—fully, exactly as you wish.
Do not explain it.
Reject any thought that stands in your way.

Live it. I know nothing. Good—zero is a brilliant foundation to begin from.

The quest for enlightenment is over; what remains is life itself—plain, immediate, inescapable. No mysticism, no detours—just the everyday rhythm of life, the ultimate pointer to here and now.

> "Now is required no incarnation of the Moon Bull, no Serpent Wisdom of the Eight Diagrams of Destiny, but a perfect human spirit alert to the needs and hopes of the heart."
>
> —Joseph Campbell, The Hero With a Thousand Faces

Thought is the brain's nonstop electrochemical chatter—patterns of firing neurons stitching perception, emotion, and habit into a running commentary that lets us predict what might happen next; memory is the residue of that firing, physical changes in neural networks laid down by experience and genetics, so every "now" arrives pre-coloured by everything that went before; the present itself is only the razor-thin slice where incoming sensory data meets that stored past and the brain instantly projects a likely future, which means pure "living in the present" in the mystical sense is neurologically impossible—attention can shift toward the fresh portion of experience, but the system that generates attention is built on memory and forecasts.

Trauma shows how hardwired this loop is: a trigger hits, the old network lights up, hormones flood, the body prepares for the danger it once survived, and the sequence feels inescapable.

Can it heal? Often you can re-encode the memory—through exposure therapy, EMDR, somatic work, medication, plain talk with someone who won't flinch—but you rarely delete it; you build parallel circuits that keep the older ones from hijacking the moment.

Genetics and upbringing set starting conditions: some nervous systems are born with hair-trigger alarms, some with thicker emotional shock absorbers. No technique rewrites the chromosome or erases the first decade of life; the "real work" is learning exactly how your particular wiring misfires and then installing guardrails—sleep discipline, exercise, breath control, social connection, sometimes pharmaceuticals—that shorten the flare-ups and widen the space between impulse and action.

The payoff isn't an eternal lotus-blossom present; it's the pragmatic freedom to notice, "Here comes the storm," ride it out, and choose the next move with a little less automatic pain. That may sound unromantic, but it's how plastic brains actually change: incrementally, through thousands of small, boring, repeatable acts that carve a calmer groove beside the old ruts.

And that, my friend, is why we're screwed. Still, the wiring in our brains keeps pushing us forward—so one more time, let's do it. Even the urge to escape is preconditioned. Behind the curtain are only puppets of imagination; the same life pulses everywhere, never quite the fantasy we picture. Life feeds on life, and there's no one to complain—just life.

Choose your own moves. The stage already echoes with the amplified voices of billionaires, influencers, and polished heroes—each hawking a script of their own. Their victories suit their wiring and their luck. Copying them is like stepping into a suit cut for another body.

Feel where you stand in this vast play. Notice the props life has handed you, the lines your history keeps whispering, the tone your nervous system favors. Act from that spot with eyes open. If you need to cry, cry. If you want to laugh, laugh. If anger comes, use its heat to hammer something useful.

Authenticity is not a slogan; it is the one force that cannot be faked because it starts inside the skin and pushes outward. Frameworks designed by the fortunate often become cages for everyone else.

Tear the cage if it does not let you breathe. Think for yourself, live as yourself, and remember that the ending is the same for every cast member. We go down, the curtain drops, and life keeps eating life. The freedom is in choosing how you dance before the lights go out.

The person beside you matters more than any boss, politician, celebrity, or distant god, because your survival depends on theirs and theirs on yours. Celebrities broadcast slogans only because someone higher up signs their checks; their propaganda serves their paymasters, not you.

Life itself runs on a different law: each cell shields the cell next to it, not out of charity but out of necessity. Never rely on those at the top—their game is not your game, their survival is not your survival. Common people can save only common people, just as one cell can safeguard only the cell beside it.

Every creature must bark from its own spot. That sound keeps it alive. If you chase celebrities to escape your life, remember their problems are not yours and their songs are not your songs. Look to politicians for a slogan and you speak words that will never feed you. Copy a celebrity's guide on how to live and you lose the game before it starts, because they are only proving they exist. Turn to religion for orders and you hand the top tier an easy tool to herd the rest. Wake up. Stand where you stand.

> Bark your own song, shout your own slogan, and remember: like a cell that thrives with the one beside it, the person next to you—and you yourself—are the true keys to this game.
>
> Always stay clear on your own role, and whenever a flashy voice jumps in to sell its story, answer firmly: "That's not my game."

Drop every master, guru, slogan, and creed — reject every scrap of bullshit. If you need a practice, just feel the breath. Notice what you avoid. Meet it. Move.

Archetypes, gods, non-duality, even these pages—cling to any of them and they calcify into dogma. Tear them up. The plainest, truest thing is life itself, and you are that life. Trust your own pulse. You are the final authority.

Like it or not, you live in this web of interconnection. Call it love, survival, or selfishness — it doesn't matter. You breathe borrowed air. You sit on someone else's labor. Even your silence costs something. But that doesn't mean you must destroy yourself for connection. Sometimes the most honest act is to be diplomatic, and sometimes, to just let people go.

So don't dress this up in slogans. Life is dynamic, not a fixed motto to chant. Don't turn it into charity, virtue, or some cause to parade. That's how people get lost, using truth as a mask, spreading noise in the name of meaning.

Stay awake. Stay direct. Stay diplomatic. Embrace the contradictions. Live it. Play the game of life. But play your game — not someone else's. Know your tools. Use what nature gave you. Let the life within you speak, stumble, dance, rage, and shine in its own pageant. That's authenticity. That's enough.

Legends say real progress begins when a brave soul snaps old chains, releases fresh life, and drives out monsters and cruel rulers so the community can grow.

But the liberator of today can turn into the tyrant of tomorrow if he will not let go of the power he has seized. True renewal demands that whatever once ruled, within us or around us, must give way. Every ending is a fresh beginning. Story after story shows a son rising against a father, yet the two are only different faces of the same living force.

Ask the pattern why it repeats and the very question burns away, carrying every answer with it. Let hope collapse yet keep dancing, and you slip beyond every system and every label. Fortune may smile or frown; the single command that remains is to flow.

The fall of the father is the self shedding its worn skin so a new shape can appear. When all figures dissolve back into primal chaos, the great wheel of the world turns again.

The separate ego never lasts. You and I are momentary illusions; the next moment will birth new questions and meanings. Thought spins tales of endless life, so we ask what lies beyond death. Remember: when the question dies, the answer dies with it, and life keeps moving on.

After that, there is no final point and no fixed center—only the living presence you feel right now, the simple fact that you are alive.

Determinism sets the stage in the shape of genes and upbringing, yet you gain a margin of freedom; choice enters in how you flow, whether doubt deepens or trust expands. Stripped of every label—nothing but breath and pulse—you move as your own current.

Nothing returns to the past—the past is gone. Let it go. Don't cling to old ideas, old beliefs, or old gods; they're just puppets in a show we once created. Beware of anyone still trapped there: it's easy to sway a crowd with yesterday's archetypes. The world will always be this rough. We're animals—maybe worse, because our imagination is vast. It's not our fault entirely; existence is heavy, and society's molds cast deep shadows inside us.

Look forward to the Age of Capricorn 4000, whatever blend of biology and machine that era invents. No one can predict it, but staring backward will never prepare us. Each epoch arrives fresh; old gods are ash, so scatter them.

Your best option is to act as your own god: move with the flow instead of trying to trap it, because flow cannot be caught. No promises, no guarantees. When the questions finally stop, the old "we" loosens and space appears for the next shape of humanity, whatever hybrid of body, mind, and machine the age demands.

No fixed answers, no fixed selves. Only the fresh pattern forming in real time. Meet it, ride it, keep flowing. We only have each other, no one else, yet we spend our time fucking one another. Yet we have to keep going, keep flowing; there is no other way.

Gather all your strength and join the dance of endless becoming —no questions, no answers, no promises, only flow. Turn your gaze backward and you fossilize; keep facing forward and you stay alive in the flow.

There is no separation between the spiritual and the material. Don't try to pin anything down; nothing holds a fixed center. The closest reality is the pulse in your own chest and the next living being you meet.

This is a single living organism. Do not grasp for hooks—there are none. Trust the life moving inside you. Act, and let outcomes unfold; life is wiser than thought. Whatever comes, stay with the itch of existence instead of running from it.

Taste every layer of being and welcome the ones still to appear. Life supports life, and that support also means life consumes life —get used to the endless ride. Release rigidity, smile, and flow. Don't look back; the past is dead. You are alive.

Close the book. Feel one honest breath. Let every idea fall away like an old knot loosening. Step into the day and meet whatever comes. Feel it fully, act with a clear heart, then let it go. That is the whole task. Life has never asked for more.

Krick, krick, krick, krick, krick.
J—R—R
Circuit complete.

Joke represents… requirement.
Don't wanna take anyone further—
It's just a burden.
There's nothing out there.
Nothing.

Joke represents requirement.
Live it. As it is. Flow.

Naked. I am naked.

Anything left? Illusion.
Darkness—illusion.
Light—illusion.
Misery? Not illusion.
Acceptance? Not illusion.
Bliss? Illusion.

The itch—
The itchiness of existence—
That's the key.
Be in it.
Just be in it.

Anything left? Illusion.

OK, tata, bye-bye, hasta la vista, ciao, ciao.

Live it. As it is. Flow.

Printed in Dunstable, United Kingdom